The Curious Public Administrator

Louis Brownlow, one of public administration's historical thinkers, once argued, "[T]he principal requirement of a good administrator is an insatiable curiosity." This book is rooted in the notion that public administrators must practice insatiable curiosity to be effective, fair, and democratic. By seeking to uncover how the world works, and therefore practicing curiosity, public administrators may be more likely to move toward evidence-based decisions, improving the efficacy and efficiency of public service. Curiosity encourages public administrators to seek answers in a caring manner and, in doing so, to empathize with the communities that they serve.

First, the book incorporates the concept of curiosity into the field of public administration. Scholarship in philosophy, business administration, social science, and other scholarly fields addresses curiosity, but public administration has yet to examine this concept in detail. This book fills that hole in the literature. Second, the book presents novel primary data on curiosity in public agencies by examining curious organizations and surveying local government officers. Third, the book presents novel primary data on how public affairs faculty view curiosity and incorporate the concept in their research and the classroom. Lastly, author William Hatcher integrates this information in the book's final chapter to present a model of administrative curiosity, focusing on creating a guide for future research and teaching. Thus, this book serves as a roadmap for developing a new doctrine of curiosity in public administration theory and practice, and it will be of enormous interest to students enrolled in public affairs courses as well as practicing public administrators and nonprofit managers.

William Hatcher is a professor of political science and public administration and the chair of the Department of Social Sciences at Augusta University. He currently serves as the co-editor-in-chief of the *Journal of Public Affairs Education*. He received both a B.S. in political science (2003) and an MPA (2004) from Georgia College and State University, and a PhD in public policy and administration from Mississippi State University (2010). Dr. Hatcher has served as a public planner and as the chair of the Board of Adjustment in Richmond, Kentucky. His research has appeared in journals, such as the *Journal of Public Affairs Education, American Journal of Public Health, American Review of Public Administration, Community Development*, and *Public Administration Quarterly*.

The Curious Public Administrator

William Hatcher

Routledge
Taylor & Francis Group

NEW YORK AND LONDON

First published 2024
by Routledge
605 Third Avenue, New York, NY 10158

and by Routledge
4 Park Square, Milton Park, Abingdon, Oxon, OX14 4RN

Routledge is an imprint of the Taylor & Francis Group, an informa business

Library of Congress Cataloging-in-Publication Data
Names: Hatcher, William (College teacher), author.
Title: The curious public administrator / William Hatcher.
Description: First edition. | New York : Routledge, 2024. | Includes
  bibliographical references and index.
Identifiers: LCCN 2023036662 (print) | LCCN 2023036663 (ebook) |
  ISBN 9781032668505 (hbk) | ISBN 9781032668819 (pbk) |
  ISBN 9781032668826 (ebk)
Subjects: LCSH: Public administration—Decision making. | Public
  administration—Psychological aspects. | Curiosity.
Classification: LCC JF1525.D4 H38 2024 (print) | LCC JF1525.D4 (ebook) |
  DDC 351—dc23/eng/20230824
LC record available at https://lccn.loc.gov/2023036662
LC ebook record available at https://lccn.loc.gov/2023036663

ISBN: 978-1-032-66850-5 (hbk)
ISBN: 978-1-032-66881-9 (pbk)
ISBN: 978-1-032-66882-6 (ebk)

DOI: 10.4324/9781032668826

Typeset in Times New Roman
by Apex CoVantage, LLC

To Jessica, Theo, and Ella. The curiosity needed to complete this book comes from their love and support.

—Will
Augusta, Georgia
July 2023

Contents

Tables

1 An Introduction to Curiosity in Public Administration

Public administrators are bureaucrats, and bureaucrats are needed to ensure that public institutions function correctly and provide effective governance. However, bureaucracy is one of the most hated words in the English language. In the United States (U.S.), the public often views bureaucrats as uncaring cogs in broken institutions, leading to a decline in public trust, which has been occurring for decades. These past few decades demonstrate the cracks in the U.S. political system, leading to political gridlock at the national level and throughout the states. Still, current public policy problems continue to abide. The U.S. political system faces the challenges of political leaders violating democratic norms, climate change, and COVID-19, making it difficult for bureaucrats to achieve the goal of effective governance. Public bureaucracies must be effective. But public administration as a scholarly discipline has failed to develop a theoretical foundation that will serve as a guidepost for theory and practice to navigate these challenging times. Scholars often look to overly complicated explanations for problems, but the simple guide may be the most impactful. And that simple guide may be an argument that public administrators need to be driven by curiosity. Administrative curiosity may be the new doctrine that helps achieve effective governance and solve the U.S. political system's challenges. And in doing so, they perhaps improve the public's trust in government and its view of bureaucrats' role in society.

A public administrator, who does not question the world around her, is a bureaucrat who is a cog in government, an administrator that fits the public's stereotype of bureaucrats. A public administrator, who is not practicing curiosity, processes policy directives and orders from superiors without evidence. Public administrators must be curious about how the administrative world works to make effective, empathetic, and equitable decisions. This argument is rooted in the intellectual tradition of public administration. As Donald Stone wrote in a *Public Administration Review* commentary from 1981, Louis Brownlow, one of the field's historical thinkers, argued, "[T]he principal requirement of a good administrator is an insatiable curiosity" (Stone, 1981, p. 507). This book is rooted in the notion that public administrators must practice insatiable curiosity to be effective, fair, and democratic. Insatiable curiosity is the book's

DOI: 10.4324/9781032668826-1

guidepost, in that the research examines curiosity in public administration and, in doing so, makes a case for the value of curiosity in managing government agencies and nonprofit organizations.

When writing a book on a topic, one must first clearly define critical concepts for the reader. Defining curiosity is necessary, because the concept is a value-based one with multiple definitions. Defining curiosity becomes even more difficult in a book that calls for the use of curiosity in the field of public administration, especially when you factor in that there are only a few articles and books that apply curiosity to public administration. Thus, for this book, the first steps are to define curiosity, introduce to the concept of administrative curiosity, and make the case why nations, our communities, and our academic discipline of public administration, need *curious public administrators*.

Googling "curiosity" produces some assorted returns from a *Fast Company* article on the "8 habits of curious people" to a site claiming, "Curiosity is the number one trait of leaders."[1] To make the first step toward making the argument for curiosity in public administration, we need to define this book's concept. Therefore, here is a short and neat definition: *Curiosity is the intellectual motivation to objectively learn how the world works* (Hatcher, 2019a, 2019b; Inan, 2013). According to Inan (2013), curiosity is seeking to answer how an "object of curiosity" is affected by the world (p. 41). Curiosity is seeking knowledge while practicing empathy about how individuals see and interact with the world. By practicing this form of curiosity, public administrators can be more effective, efficient, and fair about public administration and management decisions.

By seeking to uncover how the world works and, therefore, practicing curiosity, public administrators may be more likely to move toward evidence-based decisions, improving the efficacy and efficiency of public service. Curiosity encourages public administrators to seek answers in a caring manner and, in doing so, empathize with the communities that they serve. Thus, there should be a new doctrine for public administration theory and practice focusing on the importance of curiosity in public organizations. This book serves as a roadmap for developing this new doctrine of administrative curiosity.

The book defines curiosity; explores curiosity in other fields, such as management, psychology, medicine, and education; and applies curiosity to public administration. This book will collect data from case studies of curious public organizations (agencies and nonprofits) and curious public managers. Furthermore, I collect data by administering a survey to municipal leaders, asking about their viewpoints of curiosity in their work. The analyses and results of this survey are presented later in this book. Lastly, to learn how to align curiosity in public affairs education and future public administrators' training, the book will report a survey of public affairs faculty exploring their opinions about curiosity.

The book will advance public administration scholarship in the following ways. First, the book incorporates the concept of curiosity into the field of public administration. Scholarship in philosophy, business administration, social science, and other scholarly fields addresses curiosity, but public administration has yet to examine this concept in detail. This book fills that hole in the literature. Second, this book presents novel primary data on curiosity in public agencies by examining curious organizations and surveying local government officers. Third, this book presents novel primary data on how public affairs faculty view curiosity and incorporate the concept in their research and the classroom. Lastly, I integrate this information in this book's final chapter to present a model of administrative curiosity, focusing on creating a guide for future research and teaching.

Unpacking This Book's Definition of Curiosity

Before we accomplish these goals of the book, let us return to defining curiosity. As noted, the book defines the concept straightforwardly: *Curiosity is the intellectual motivation to learn objectively how the world works.* I want to unpack this definition to discuss how administrative curiosity may be the foundation for a new doctrine of public administration. First, what is meant by *intellectual motivation*? This component of the definition focuses on administrators being driven by an intellectual focus. It is a motivation fueled by wanting to know how the world works, not by pure self-interest, as described by a rational choice view of incentives (Neumann & Ritz, 2015). Within the public administration literature, there has been a conflict between the self-interest explanation of motivation put forth by the New Public Management school of thought and the "self-sacrificing" view of motivation put forth primarily through Perry's (1996) public service motivation (PSM) (Vandenabeele, 2007). For public administrators, curiosity is being driven by a self-sacrificing search for knowledge to build intellectual understanding, not for pure gain but for the sake of knowing something.

Next, what is meant by *to learn objectivity*? While recognizing the limitations of objectivity (Riccucci, 2010), the book's definition of curiosity considers the assumption that decision-makers must attempt to employ detachment to understand how the world works. They do this by recognizing biases. By acknowledging biases upfront, curious thinkers can acknowledge when their subjective thinking influences their search for how the world works. The lack of foresight leading up to the collapse of an earthen dam on the Teton River in 1975 illustrates the importance of public administrators recognizing their biases and collecting information for numerous individuals, even low-level employees. In an excellent article titled "Grout," Schmidt (1993) details how public managers did not foresee the collapse of the damn, because they were listening to experts, an inherent bias toward expertise, instead of on the ground, low-level employees who communicated that there was something wrong with the damn. Seeking to learn how the world works through curiosity may have pushed the managers to talk with all affected parties instead of primarily experts who turned out to be wrong.

Lastly, what is meant by *how the world works*? This part of the definition may be the easiest part to unpack. The phrase refers to empirical evidence describing why phenomena occur. While this may be the easiest to unpack, it is the goal of curious thinking and decision-making. The goal is to construct explanations and descriptions of the outcomes and features of the world around us. Regarding curiosity in administration, the focus is on how the public administrative world works. Throughout this book, we will discuss *how the public administrative world works*, which is a phrase that encompasses many, many parts of the overall world around us.

As we will discuss in greater detail in this book, psychology is perhaps the field that has examined curiosity in greater detail. The field's definition of the concept differs somewhat from the description that I have created for public administration. In psychology, curiosity, according to Litman and Spielberger (2003), "is broadly defined as a desire for acquiring new knowledge and new sensory experience that motivates exploratory behavior" (p. 77). The first part of this definition relates to the one I use in this book. The psychological definition of curiosity, which is mainly the drive to acquire new knowledge, influences this book's definition. Moreover, philosophy's view of curiosity (Inan, 2013), in particular the focus on intellectual motivation, is embedded in this book's definition of curiosity. And again, this definition is: *Curiosity is the intellectual motivation to learn objective how the world works.*

Public administrators need to follow this simple definition of curiosity in decision-making. By doing this, public administrators may help improve government trust. Curiosity drives administrators to be more empathetic, caring, kind, and effective. Curiosity may lead administrators to make evidence-based decisions. Thus, the curious public administrator should be a new normative doctrine to guide public administration.

Toward a New Doctrine of the Curious Public Administrator

As I recounted in an editorial in *Public Integrity* (2019b), the germ of the idea for the curious public administrator came from reading Atul Gawande's (2018) description of his commencement address to graduates of the School of Medicine at UCLA. Gawande discussed how he used curiosity in medical treatment to gain cooperation from a patient guilty of an especially vile crime. By talking with the patient and seeking answers to questions, Gawande developed an effective treatment for the patient. By talking and learning, we may empathize and demonstrate care through which we solve public problems through the following:

1. Fostering public participation

Curious public administrators want to encourage public input in governance decisions, because they seek to know how the world works, and public participation supplies them with evidence. Local government administrators often shy away from public participation, because they lose control over the process. Administrators are not confident in the public's ability to provide guidance (Hatcher, 2015). However, the curious public administrator understands that the communities served are the closest individuals to the frontlines of public policy implementation. Such proximity produces contextual knowledge and helps build evidence for decisions. And curious public administrators practice empathy, making them more likely to develop meaningful interactions with the public.

2. Practicing empathy

As with Gawande's caring for a challenging patient, the curious public administrator will be more likely to practice empathy than the typical public administrator by asking questions about the administrative world. Through practicing empathy, public administrators' work is more effective and fair. As Edlins (2019) describes, empathy in public administration allows public servants to "balance technical skills with emotional competency," which will increase understanding and improve interactions between the public and the administrative state (p. 6). Moreover, "a culture of empathy" in public organizations builds "relational public administration" and, in doing so, improves public service (Dolamore, 2019, p. 1). It appears that public administration as a field is teaching empathy. Still, as Edlins and Dolamore (2018) found from their survey of faculty program directors, there needs to be more focus on empathy in our curricula and courses. This work can be done by encouraging curiosity in public administration, because empathy builds meaningful interactions between the public and government, leading to understanding and, hopefully, more caring organizations.

3. Building *Caring Organizations*

Through practicing empathy, the curious public administrator will help build "caring organizations" where managers seek to implement evidence-based decisions that advance their organizations' missions and support their employees. Caring organizations recognize that their missions depend on their employees' health and welfare. Eldor (2018) described them as "compassionated organizations," where supervisors promote "compassionate feelings such as affection, generosity, caring, and tenderness" (p. 86). Through a large, longitudinal study of civil servants in Israel, Eldor (2018) found that employees with compassionate supervisors were less likely to suffer from burnout and were likely to be more effective at their jobs than employees with supervisors who did not promote compassionate feelings. The research is a potent reminder of the importance of caring and compassion in organizations, especially public ones, promoting excellence and ensuring employee well-being. Eldor's (2017) research is a cornerstone of this book's data analysis, explored in later chapters.

Additionally, the affective events theory (AET) can help us understand why caring organizations are essential to the people served by public organizations and the employees working for public organizations. AET posits that workplace events have an emotional influence on employees and affect their health and work productivity (Wegge et al., 2006). AET is utilized as a framework to understand caring organizations and curiosity in public administration. By recognizing that events affect emotions and affect employees and their work, public administration can make institutions strive for effectiveness and social equity and hopefully repair public trust.

4. Repairing public trust in government

Curious public administrators build empathy and caring organizations throughout the U.S. political system. Government, therefore, will be more effective, caring, and democratic. With that, people will be more likely to trust public institutions again than they are likely to distrust the nation's public institutions' current dilapidated state. As Kettl (2018) argues, positive interactions between public officials and the public, what is termed individual-level or "retail-level" trust, may rebuild overall trust in government. Being curious, empathic, and caring, looking to involve the public in decision-making leads to positive interactions and rebuilding trust. Academic programs in public affairs can teach these important concepts and their relationship with improving trust (Kettl, 2018).

Thus, trust, empathy, caring, and evidence are the guideposts of the curious public administrator. Curious public administrators seek to know how the world works and will look for evidence. Accordingly, they will be more inclined to encourage public participation, and through developing relational bonds with the public, they are empathic. Organizations with curious and empathic administrators are caring, and having caring public organizations will help repair trust in government and make our institutions more democratic. The preceding chapters discuss how we can achieve these goals.

Plan for the Book

The following is the plan for how this book will explore curiosity in public administration.

The next chapter will define and align curiosity by reviewing the scholarly literature on the topic. The review describes curiosity by examining literature from philosophy, medicine, education, management, and other fields. This chapter traces the history of the concept among philosophers, focuses on curiosity's epistemic value, and recognizes potential vices of curiosity. Next, this chapter examines how curiosity plays a role in psychology, management, philosophy, health, and social sciences. The culmination of this review will be a definition of curiosity and expanding this concept to administrative curiosity.

The book's third chapter builds on the literature review in Chapter 2 by discussing how the curiosity findings in other scholarly fields construct an administrative doctrine for our field of public administration. This chapter traces the concept of curiosity throughout the works of public administration thinkers and schools of thought. I discuss the views on curiosity espoused by Max Weber, Frederick Taylor, Mary Parker Follett, Dwight Waldo, Herbert Simon, and modern public administration scholars. Furthermore, this chapter will examine the placement of curiosity in public administration schools of thought, such as New Public Administration, New Public Management, network analysis, and the literature on bureaucratic hurdles. I discuss how the first municipal bureaus of research and the ideas of Mary Parker Follett demonstrated curiosity. Guy et al.'s (2014) work on emotional labor and ethical decision-making is examined through the lens of curiosity, along with recent work on empathy in public administration. Moreover, Stivers's (2002) distinction of "settlement women" being more empathic and compassionate than "bureau men" is explored as a theoretical foundation in Chapter 3. This chapter concludes with a model of administrative curiosity.

The book examines curiosity among public administrators by collecting survey data on city managers/administrators, curiosity among faculty in public affairs programs by collecting survey data from them, and curiosity in organizations by using a case study of federal agencies.

Chapters 4 and 5 contribute to the field's literature by collecting primary data about curiosity in public administration practice, scholarship, and teaching. Chapter 4 examines the concept of curiosity in public administration practice by surveying city managers and administrators. This chapter details the results of a survey administered by email to the chief administrative officers in U.S. cities with populations greater than 10,000 people. The chief administrative officers of approximately 2,500 cities throughout the nation will receive the survey. The survey will be the first nationwide attempt to gather information on how city managers and administrators view and practice the concept of curiosity in their work. The survey instrument will ask the municipal managers to define curiosity and discuss how curiosity affects their work. The survey instrument will include control questions to collect data regarding the cities' socioeconomic characteristics and the participating public managers, the public managers' educational backgrounds, and the managers' demographics. The data are analyzed by descriptive statistics, content analysis of open-ended questions, crosstabs, factor analysis, and regression.

Chapter 5 collects primary data from researchers and instructors who teach in NASPAA member programs of public affairs. The survey instrument asks for the faculty's viewpoints regarding researching the concept of curiosity and how to teach curiosity in public affairs programs. The survey will be emailed to over 2,700 faculty in the NASPAA member schools and public affairs programs. As noted, the survey will ask the public affairs faculty their viewpoint on curiosity, their opinions about the importance of curiosity to public administration, and their ideas about instruction methods to illustrate the concept. The survey will also include control questions asking the faculty their academic rank, tenure status, educational background, career experience as practitioners, and demographics. Additionally, the instrument will consist of questions about the programs where the faculty teach, such as the number of students, the program's concentrations, and whether the program is housed in a research institution. The survey data is analyzed by descriptive statistics, content analysis of open-ended questions, crosstabs, factor analysis, and regression.

Chapter 6 examines curiosity in organizations. Mission-orientated organizations are effective in serving the public (Goodsell, 2010). Chapter 4 profiles mission-orientated public agencies to determine if they demonstrate the features of curiosity, such as focusing on evidence in decision-making and empathy in service. This chapter examines curiosity in public agencies studied by Goodsell (2010) in *Mission Mystique*. The profiles included in this chapter are not complete case studies of the agencies. Instead, the profiles identify curiosity features in these agencies, such as the concern for advancing science in the U.S. Centers for Disease Control and Prevention and the quality of empathy in the U.S. Peace Corps. This chapter will profile curiosity in these agencies by analyzing mission statements, performance assessments, and other publicly available documents.

The book concludes with a presentation of the new doctrine of public administration. This chapter compiles the information gathered throughout the text into a framework to help guide practitioners, scholars, and instructors toward using administrative curiosity in their work. This chapter will cover how public administration scholars can teach and research administrative curiosity.

Concluding Thoughts

As of the writing of this book, the U.S. is facing multiple crises, including a deadly pandemic that is one of the top death events in the nation's history; former president Trump's damage to the nation's constitutional system; the looming catastrophe from global warming; an economy that leaves many in poverty and consolidates wealth in the hands of a few; and many other struggles that potentially could undo the nation's experiment into democratic governance. The motivation to learn how the world works in a manner that promotes empathy and caring is needed more than ever. Curiosity needs to be the defining guide for decision-making in the public sphere. The concept gives public administrators a rubric to help the nation's bureaucracies make empathic, caring, and effective decisions. The nation depends on this.

Let us explore what scholars know about curiosity and how we can use the concept to build participation, empathy, trust, and caring to ensure effective and democratic public administration.

Note

1 The reader is encouraged to Google curiosity at the time that she is reading this book. The results may have changed.

References

Dolamore, S. (2019). Detecting empathy in public organizations: Creating a more relational public administration. *Administrative Theory & Praxis*, 1–24.

Edlins, M. (2019). Developing a model of empathy for public administration. *Administrative Theory & Praxis*, 1–20.

Edlins, M., & Dolamore, S. (2018). Ready to serve the public? The role of empathy in public service education programs. *Journal of Public Affairs Education*, *24*(3), 300–320.

Eldor, L. (2018). Public service sector: The compassionate workplace—The effect of compassion and stress on employee engagement, burnout, and performance. *Journal of Public Administration Research and Theory*, *28*(1), 86–103.

Gawande, A. (2018, June 2). Curiosity and what equality really means. *The New Yorker.* Retrieved from www.newyorker.com/news/news-desk/curiosity-and-the-prisoner.

Goodsell, C. T. (2010). *Mission mystique: Belief systems in public agencies.* Sage.

Guy, M. E., Newman, M. A., & Mastracci, S. H. (2014). *Emotional labor: Putting the service in public service: Putting the service in public service.* Routledge.

Hatcher, W. (2015). The efficacy of public participation in municipal budgeting: An exploratory survey of officials in government finance officers association's award-winning cities. *Public Administration Quarterly*, *39*(4), 645–663.

Hatcher, W. (2019a). Teaching curiosity in public affairs programs. *Teaching Public Administration*, *37*(3), 365–375.

Hatcher, W. (2019b). The curious public administrator: The new administrative doctrine. *Public Integrity*, *21*(3), 225–228.

Inan, I. (2013). *The philosophy of curiosity.* Routledge.

Kettl, D. F. (2018). Earning trust in government. *Journal of Public Affairs Education*, *24*(3), 295–299.

Litman, J. A., & Spielberger, C. D. (2003). Measuring epistemic curiosity and its diversive and specific components. *Journal of Personality Assessment*, *80*(1), 75–86.

Neumann, O., & Ritz, A. (2015). Public service motivation and rational choice modelling. *Public Money & Management*, *35*(5), 365–370.

Perry, J. L. (1996). Measuring public service motivation: An assessment of construct reliability and validity. *Journal of Public Administration Research and Theory*, *6*(1), 5–22.

Riccucci, N. M. (2010). *Public administration: Traditions of inquiry and philosophies of knowledge.* Georgetown University Press.

Schmidt, M. R. (1993). Grout: Alternative kinds of knowledge and why they are ignored. *Public Administration Review*, *53*(6), 525–530.

Stivers, C. M. (2002). *Bureau men, settlement women: Constructing public administration in the progressive era*. University Press of Kansas.

Stone, D. C. (1981). Innovative organizations require innovative managers. *Public Administration Review, 41*(5), 507–513.

Vandenabeele, W. (2007). Toward a public administration theory of public service motivation: An institutional approach. *Public Management Review, 9*(4), 545–556.

Wegge, J., Dick, R. V., Fisher, G. K., West, M. A., & Dawson, J. F. (2006). A test of basic assumptions of Affective Events Theory (AET) in call centre work 1. *British Journal of Management, 17*(3), 237–254.

2 Defining and Aligning Curiosity

This chapter defines and aligns administrative curiosity by reviewing the scholarly literature on the topic. The discussion relies on the definition of curiosity constructed in Chapter 1, and to recap, this definition is: *Curiosity is the intellectual motivation to learn objectively how the world works.* But as noted, the research in public administration has been limited. Thus, to fully define and align administrative curiosity, this chapter reviews a broad collection of scholarly literature from philosophy, medicine, sociology, psychology, management, economics, political science, and of course, the related work in public affairs, policy, and administration. This chapter traces the history of the concept among philosophers, focuses on curiosity's epistemic value, and recognizes potential vices of curiosity. Next, this chapter examines curiosity in psychology, management, philosophy, health, and social sciences. The culmination of this review will be a definition of curiosity and expanding this concept to administrative curiosity.

But first, I would like to develop further my argument for why curiosity matters for organizations. Before we explore the scholarly literature on the concept, it will be helpful to present the characteristics of curious organizations. Most of the scholarly work on curiosity is from research conducted in the private sector, so we must start our discussion focusing on the concept in private organizations. In the *Harvard Business Review*, Gino (2018) detailed the results of her research on curiosity in business. According to those findings, she found curious workers more productive, and organizations with curious workers have less group conflict, better-functioning communications, and overall better team performance than organizations with employees not practicing curiosity (Gino, 2018).

Moreover, Gino identified practices that can help organizations cultivate curiosity. These practices are features that organizations need to be considered curious organizations. The practices are hiring curious employees, promoting inquisitiveness, encouraging learning goals, freeing employees to explore, and creating days or time for exploration (Gino, 2018). Thus, curious organizations have these five features. This chapter will use these five features to define and align with a curious public administrator. First, let us explore the curiosity

DOI: 10.4324/9781032668826-2

literature in psychology and philosophy as well as how we identify curious individuals.

Identifying Curiosity and Curious Individuals

What makes individuals curious? The literature in two disciplines—psychology and philosophy—can help us answer this question. The answer is given in two parts: descriptive, where psychology can help us, and normative, where philosophy plays a role in our quest to answer the question, What makes individuals curious? By descriptive, I mean defining how the world works and what motivates individuals to be curious; by normative, I mean defining how the world ought to work and the philosophical underpinnings of curiosity. Psychology is perhaps the best discipline to consult because of the field's long history of studying the concept. And the literature on curiosity in psychology is mature, with numerous quality studies using many tested instruments going back to the end of the 1800s (James, 2007). In a seminal review, Loewenstein (1994) organized the literature on curiosity into two waves. The first wave of studies was concerned with defining curiosity and developing a theory of the concept to test. The second wave included studies on how to measure curiosity. Thus, curiosity has been studied empirically by defining the idea and then seeking how to measure it. I do not explore all this literature as part of this chapter. Another *Harvard Business Review* article can help us summarize how psychology has defined curiosity.

Kashdan and colleagues (2018) reviewed psychology's literature and identified the "five dimensions of curiosity." The five dimensions are as follows:

1. Deprivation of sensitivity or realizing "a gap in knowledge."
2. Joyous exploration or enjoying learning how the world works.
3. Social curiosity or seeking to learn from others through interactions.
4. Stress tolerance or being open to dealing with the frustration that may come from new things.
5. Thrill-seeking or seeking to take risks.

(p. 58–60)

In a study of 508 adults, researchers found support for the five dimensions of curiosity. Using this framework, the authors identified "found distinct curious people," including "The Fascinated (28%) of the sample, Problem Solvers (28%), Empathizers (25%), and Avoiders (19%)" (Kashdan et al., 2018, p. 130). The researchers used factor analysis of the sample's responses to numerous questionnaires. According to research, the *Fascinated* group consists of individuals who are highly educated, outgoing, and able to deal with stressful situations. *Problem Solvers* value independence and focus on dealing with issues rather than seeking social support. The *Empathizers* care greatly about social connections but are self-identified as easily stressed. Lastly, *Avoiders* were the least curious individuals in the sample, with the lowest socioeconomic characteristics, the least social, and the most stressed.

Curiosity depends on an individual's assumptions that they have a "knowledge gap" on a topic, enjoy learning and asking questions, are to various degrees social in nature, manage stress, and sometimes seek thrills and take chances. So far, our exploration of curiosity and public administration has treated the concept as entirely positive. On the other hand, the psychology literature gives us pause, particularly the finding that curious individuals may take undue risks in seeking thrills (Birenbaum et al., 2019). This finding raises the need to be more cautious in our treatment of curiosity, and turning to normative writing and philosophy can help us garner that appreciation.

Normative Views of Curiosity

While research in the social sciences and other fields on curiosity can help us lay the groundwork for the empirical (i.e., how the world actually works) defining and aligning of curiosity, philosophy most likely helps us with the normative (i.e., how the world ought to be) foundation of the concept. Why?

Philosophy can help us not only with the epistemic value of curiosity but also with its vices. The literature in philosophy can help explain the benefits of curiosity and the possible dangers. For instance, as noted, a potential vice identified by psychology is that curious individuals may be too open to risk, putting them in physical danger or economically unstable situations (Inan, 2013). Moreover, curiosity about knowing morbid and inappropriate information about others is often a vice (Baumgarten, 2001). Such seeking of knowledge may violate social norms and boundaries that individuals may want to be kept in place.

Additionally, idle curiosity, where one seeks answers to questions that may be unimportant, could be a vice for individuals (Baumgarten, 2001). Ancient philosophy often viewed curiosity as invoking disorder in consistent searching for novelty, and for instance, Augustine thought of curiosity as a "vulgar" interruption from "prayer and meditation" (Walsh, 1988, p. 84). Moreover, curiosity can lead to invasions of privacy by individuals seeking to learn more and focus on their interests (Manson, 2012).

A macro-level vice may be that the distribution of curiosity in a society may be unequal. Zurn (2021) examines curiosity's relationship to politics and power and argues that those who explore how the world works, or practice curiosity, are often individuals with power within a society. However, a virtue of curiosity in Zurn's (2021) thesis is that those on the dissenting side of power structures are also likely to practice curiosity to right economic, political, and social wrongs. Furthermore, curiosity leads to empathy. Through sociable curiosity, people become interested in learning more about others and developing relational curiosity, encouraging empathy among individuals and perhaps power structures (Phillips, 2016).

Let us again revisit how we define curiosity and its epistemic value with help from the field of philosophy. In his appropriately titled book, *The Philosophy of Curiosity*, Inan (2013) describes curiosity as meeting the following features. First, curiosity is seeking to obtain new knowledge about some piece of how the world works. Often this is a focus on asking questions and seeking answers to build empirical explanations of the phenomenon. Second, to be truly curious, one needs to identify their ignorance about parts of the world. Based on this, a curious person may not be as susceptible to the Dunning-Kruger Effect. The effect holds that unskilled individuals view their knowledge in an area as more significant than that of an individual who is skilled in the specific area (Dunning, 2011). A curious person can recognize when they are ignorant and unskilled in an area of knowledge to ask empirical questions and find answers. Thus, lastly, Inan holds that curiosity is about accepting and dispelling ignorance about the world. To be curious, one must recognize a lack of knowledge, but next, one also must seek to remedy that deficiency.

The journalist Michael Lewis has a history of writing books about individuals who fit Inan's (2013) philosophy of curiosity. In *Moneyball*, Lewis (2003) explores Billy Bean as general manager of the Oakland Athletics to help make the team competitive by focusing on the use of statistical analysis in baseball and moving away from relying entirely on perceptional decision-making, not always rooted in evidence. In *The Big Short*, Lewis (2010) explored those who successfully predicted the housing market crash before the Great Recession of 2008. In two more recent books, *The Fifth Risk* (2018) and *The Premonition* (2021), Lewis focused on curious individuals in government who identified problems with Trump administration (*The Fifth Risk*) and who mapped out the social distance components of pandemic prevention before the COVID-19 pandemic (*The Premonition*). In the latter book, Lewis examines public health officer Dr. Charity Dean's diligent efforts to get the state of California to address the COVID-19 threat in the early days of the pandemic. She seeks to dispel ignorance in her public health role. From Billy Bean in *Moneyball* to Charity Dean in *The Premonition*, there is a commonality among the individuals profiled by Lewis. The underlying factor is that they practice curiosity, as Inan (2013) described. They recognize when they do not know something about the world, ask questions to learn, and seek to build evidence to dispel their ignorance. From a normative standpoint in public administration, this sounds like a quality trait for a bureaucrat or public manager.

But let us move forward from normative views of philosophy to focus on how the concept works in the real world. And with this, ask a question, what are the empirical findings regarding curiosity? To answer, let us return to psychology and empirical fields of study.

Defining and Aligning Curiosity in Fields of Study

What do we empirically know about curiosity? First, we know the concept has vices and virtues (Loewenstein, 1994). For instance, empirical research demonstrates that the thrill-seeking aspect of curiosity may be a vice in that it pushes individuals toward risky decisions (Kashdan et al., 2018; Kashdan et al. 2020a, 2020b), or what is often described through the cliché "curiosity killed the cat" vice of the concept. On the other hand, the curious individuals' drive to know the world is often a benefit for decision-making and the overall health of organizations. This book focuses on public organizations and the virtue of curiosity in the public sector. Recent research on curiosity in private workplaces demonstrates the virtues of the concept by showing that curious individuals are "high performing, satisfied individuals in the workplace" (Kashdan et al., 2020, p. 109717).

Additionally, curiosity is a component of the "social aspects of knowledge production," as described in the field of sociology (Bineth, 2020, p. 13). Such knowledge production produces a "social construction of reality," or what we perceive as the world around us is influenced by our social norms, values, traditions, and other sociological variables (Berger & Luckmann, 1966). Through curiosity, one applies these social constructs to define how the world around them works. Still, one can also transcend those constraints of social norms, values, and traditions and gather information about reality. Appreciating how curiosity intersects with the social production of knowledge and sociology gives us a clearer picture of the concept and how it may affect public administration.

Next, curiosity is a political variable. Again, drawing from *Curiosity and Power* by Zurn (2021), curiosity is political because of the questions allowed in society and the types of lifestyles accepted. Curiosity is a product of those who are in power, but on the other hand, the power of curiosity can deconstruct political institutions and lead to new political movements. Dissenters, reformers, and others against a current political status quo start changing or even deconstructing that power structure by first questioning it and engaging in curious behavior. Thus, political power structures limit curiosity and may be the leading force against power in societies and nations.

Combining curiosity as a sociological and political variable is illustrated in the arguments of Stagl's (1995) *A History of Curiosity*. In the book, Stagl demonstrates how curiosity is the glue of early social research and the foundation of the current social science disciplines, such as sociology, political science, and other "socio-cultural sciences" (p. 2). To Stagl, the early formation of these disciplines had in common the practice of curiosity as being "the urge to explore unknown situations" and being a "feature of world-openness" (p. 2). Hence, social research partly developed from the desire for those to know previously unknown information. Moreover, curiosity has more influence in an open or not politically limited society, allowing freedom to ask questions and seek knowledge, even if that information threatens power structures.

Curiosity is essential in how we learn about the world and question reality and power structures, but the concept is a critical component of how we teach and educate one another about the world and its socio-political features. The scholarship of teaching and learning typically views curiosity as a tool to help motivate learners or students by sparking their interest in particular subjects (Pluck & Johnson, 2011; Rossing & Long, 1981). Then the question is: Can curiosity be taught? Guthrie (2009) asked this question, and through practice and curiosity to ask the question, he found that research shows that certain factors "enhance curiosity" (p. 66). Here is Guthrie's (2009) review of the literature on teaching curiosity:

> People appear to become more curious when they are in a good mood (Murray et al., 1990; Hirt et al., 1996), when working with others (Isaac et al., 1999; Sansone & Thoman, 2005), and when participating in novel or complex activities that they nonetheless find comprehensible (Silvia, 2005, 2006, 2008).
>
> (Guthrie, 2009, p. 66)

Thus, people can become more curious, learn the skill, be in a good mood, practice collegiality in their interpersonal relationships, and explore new and multifaceted ideas (Guthrie, 2009).

Based on these findings, curiosity is about ideas, but it is also social. Engel (2011) argues this point in an essay on curiosity in children. According to Engel, curiosity is developed early in life and is the product of social interactions among children, often in a classroom setting. Hence, the environmental, social, and learning features of classrooms matter in encouraging curiosity in individuals. Engel argues that teaching to exams and installing too many routines in teaching (an over-bureaucratization of education) hamper curiosity. Based on the literature on the teaching and learning of curiosity, it seems that curiosity sparks early in one's life. Still, knowing what causes individuals to pique their curiosity can encourage the drive for inquiry.

Curiosity occurs at the intersection of teaching and medicine. As Dyche and Epstein (2011) write, "For doctors, curiosity is fundamental to understanding each patient's unique experience of illness" (p. 663). My interest in curiosity was sparked, as noted in Chapter 1, by Atul Gawande's essay discussing how practicing curiosity makes him a better doctor. To Gawande, being curious about the health of a patient, who committed a horrible crime, helped him treat the individual. It was not about knowing more about the patient. It was about learning more about the patient's health. The drive to know more is objective and encourages seeking knowledge from places one would not usually look. As Dyche and Epstein (2011) argue, "[C]uriosity is fundamental to understanding each patient's unique experience of illness, building respectful relationships with patients, deepening self-awareness, supporting clinical reasoning, avoiding premature closure and encouraging lifelong learning" (p. 663). Dyche and

Epstein (2011) argue that curiosity is learned by pushing medical students to take responsibility for their learning.

Measuring Curiosity

Evidence that curiosity can be learned leads us to questions of how research measures curiosity in the first place. Focusing on measuring curiosity is needed to help us define the concept, build a theory for public administration, and test it. This book attempts to accomplish these three goals. To do so, we need to briefly discuss the literature on measuring curiosity. As Litman and Spielberger (2003) note in their literature review, a wealth of research on measuring curiosity exists. Litman and Spielberger (2003), in particular, focused on measuring epistemic curiosity and perceptual curiosity. Epistemic curiosity is the need to know how something about the world works, and perceptual curiosity is being interested in something new that increases interest in learning more about other phenomena (Berlyne, 1954, 1957). In their study, Litman and Spielberger administered a survey instrument to undergraduate students. The instrument contained 16 items focusing on perceptual curiosity developed by Collins (1996) and 40 items focusing on epistemic curiosity development by Berlyne (1954). The authors found a host of variables, including gender, to influence curiosity.

Over the years, other scholars have attempted to build measures of curiosity. Working from the idea that curiosity is focused on knowing about many subjects (breadth) and narrowing knowledge to one specific subject (depth), Ainley (1987) and Fulcher (2004) have worked toward developing a curiosity index. The index, along with the instruments developed by researchers like Litman and Spielberger (2003), is essential to the book's research on how adults learn and use that learning in administrative settings. Accordingly, ideas from educational theory can help us develop a foundation for the book research. In an essay on curiosity in educational theory, Schmitt and Lahroodi (2008) identify "sources" of curiosity: (1) curiosity builds understanding; (2) curiosity is driven by subjects that people already "have a practical or epistemic interest"; and (3) curiosity is not limited to the interest of individuals. (p. 125). Thus, curiosity differs from wonder, in that curiosity is focused on learning broadly and not driven solely by the enjoyment of a topic (Opdal, 2001).

I want to stress again that the focus of this book is taking the ideas of curiosity and applying the concepts to public administration. Later in the book, we will return to measuring curiosity. We use the instruments discussed in this section to build the book's surveys of local government officials and faculty in public administration.

But lastly, while it is not an empirical analysis in the strict sense, I think a book on curiosity would not be complete without mentioning one of fiction's most curious characters, Sherlock Holmes. In writing the character of Holmes, Conan Doyle often referred to the "curious case" of the various investigations by Holmes and his sidekick Watson. A potential vice of curiosity is that it will lead one to explore everything at the risk of not learning essential knowledge for their work, job, and other aspects of their lives. Such an expansion of practice of curiosity limits the drive for learning. In other words, how do decision-makers be curious while tuning out the noise of wanting to know everything about all? Robertson (2012) discusses how Sherlock Holmes could use precision in his curiosity to turn down the noise and focus on the evidence and information that is most important to his curious cases.

Later in this book, we will discuss how public administrators need to practice this focused curiosity to know more about how their administrative worlds work, but for now, let us move into what we know in public administration about curiosity and areas related to the concept. As Holmes would say, "The game is afoot!"

Next Steps: Defining and Aligning Curiosity in Public Administration

An underlying argument of this book is that, in organizations, individuals practicing curiosity will lead to effective "collective action" (Harrison, 2011). In the following chapter, we will construct a theory of curiosity for public administration. Still, while focusing on aligning and defining curiosity, which is the subject of this current chapter, we need to address some of the questions necessary for understanding curiosity in the field of public administration. Some of those questions are as follows:

1. How should we define curiosity in public administration? The proceeding chapter and this one define curiosity for the field.
2. How does curiosity interact with other values important to public administration? How does curiosity interact with efficiency, effectiveness, fairness, efforts for social equity, and different core values of public administration?
3. How does curiosity interact with critical public service values and motivations?
4. How does curiosity interact with other values that are not considered core components of public administration but are discussed in our field? How does it interact with ambition, innovation, entrepreneurialism, and others?
5. How does curiosity fit in the primary schools of thought in public administration?
6. How does the curiosity of an individual administrator affect the importance of the "public" in public administration?

Chapter 3 positions curiosity in public administration and develops a theory of the curious public administrator. Before we move on to that chapter, though, I would like to end this one by discussing how curiosity fits in the schools of thought in public administration (Frederickson et al., 2018; Henry,

1975). Over the past 100 years, theory development within public administration has been a disjointed process, with theoretical ideas taken from multiple disciplines. Still, throughout this evolution, there are a few schools of thought that can be identified. First, early public administration, starting in the late 1800s and into the Progressive Movement, mainly focused on promoting efficiency and examining the influence of partisan politics on administration (McDonald, 2010). Second, public administration focused on principles, starting around the New Deal in the U.S., pushed for research on how critical tasks are performed by administrators, such as budgeting, planning, and personnel management. Third, public administration, starting around World War II with the influence of Herbert Simon, moved toward examining how individuals make decisions within organizations. In the mid-1900s, public administration splintered into numerous schools of thought, including New Public Management, New Public Administration, decision theory, theory of bureaucratic politics, and other areas of inquiry. Recently, the field expanded to include network governance, democratic theory, social equity, representative bureaucracy, administrative burdens (Herd & Moynihan, 2019), and other theories (Frederickson et al., 2018).

Throughout this development of theory, little research, as noted earlier in this book, seeks to explain and describe curiosity in public administration. However, a commonality in the theories of public administration is the striving to be both descriptive and normative (Frederickson et al., 2018). Theory in the field of public administration is descriptive, in that scholars seek to know how the world actually works. It is normative in that scholars also want to learn how to make the world better, which in our field is done by improving public administration. Curiosity drives the search for descriptive and normative explanations of public administration, and while they may not acknowledge it, the drive to question and learn about the world is rooted in the work of public servants seeking to better their communities, organizations, states, and nation. Moving forward, we will next build an administrative theory of curiosity in Chapter 3, and in later chapters, we will test that theory, which is an exercise of curiosity itself.

References

Ainley, M. D. (1987). The factor structure of curiosity measures: Breadth and depth of interest curiosity styles. *Australian Journal of Psychology, 39*(1), 53–59.

Baumgarten, E. (2001). Curiosity as a moral virtue. *International Journal of Applied Philosophy, 15*(2), 169–184.

Berger, P. L., Berger, P. L., & Luckmann, T. (1966). *The social construction of reality: A treatise in the sociology of knowledge.* Anchor.

Berlyne, D. E. (1954). An experimental study of human curiosity. *British Journal of Psychology, 45*(4), 256.

Berlyne, D. E. (1957). Conflict and information-theory variables as determinants of human perceptual curiosity. *Journal of Experimental Psychology, 53*(6), 399.

Bineth, A. (2020). *Towards a sociology of curiosity* [Doctoral dissertation, Central European University].

Birenbaum, M., Alhija, F. N. A., Shilton, H., Kimron, H., Rosanski, R., & Shahor, N. (2019). A further look at the five-dimensional curiosity construct. *Personality and Individual Differences, 149*, 57–65.

Collins, R. P. (1996). *Identification of perceptual curiosity as a psychological construct: Development of the perceptual curiosity scale* [Unpublished master's thesis]. University of South Florida.

Dunning, D. (2011). The Dunning–Kruger effect: On being ignorant of one's own ignorance. In *Advances in experimental social psychology* (Vol. 44, pp. 247–296). Academic Press.

Dyche, L., & Epstein, R. M. (2011). Curiosity and medical education. *Medical Education, 45*(7), 663–668.

Engel, S. (2011). Children's need to know: Curiosity in schools. *Harvard Educational Review, 81*(4), 625–645.

Frederickson, H. G., Smith, K. B., Larimer, C. W., & Licari, M. J. (2018). *The public administration theory primer*. Routledge.

Fulcher, K. H. (2004). *Towards measuring lifelong learning: The curiosity index* [Doctoral dissertation, ProQuest Information & Learning].

Gino, F. (2018, September-October). Why curiosity matters? *Harvard Business Review*, pp. 47–61.

Guthrie, C. (2009). I'm curious: Can we teach curiosity? In C. Honeyman, J. Coben & G. De Palo (Eds.), *Rethinking negotiation teaching: Innovations for context and culture*. DRI Press, Hamline University, Saint Paul, MN. (pp. 63–70).

Harrison, S. (2011). Organizing the cat? Generative aspects of curiosity in organizational life. In G. M. Spreitzer & K. S. Cameron (Eds.), *The Oxford handbook of positive organizational scholarship*. Oxford University Press.

Henry, N. (1975). Paradigms of public administration. *Public Administration Review, 35*(4), 378–386.

Herd, P., & Moynihan, D. P. (2019). *Administrative burden: Policymaking by other means*. Russell Sage Foundation.

Hirt, E. R., Melton, R. J., McDonald, H. E., & Harackiewicz, J. M. (1996). Processing goals, task interest, and the mood-performance relationship: A mediational analysis. *Journal of Personality and Social Psychology, 71*(2), 245–261.

Inan, I. (2013). *The philosophy of curiosity*. Routledge.

Isaac, J. D., Sansone, C., & Smith, J. (1999). Other people as a source of interest in an activity. *Journal of Experimental Social Psychology, 35*(3), 239–265.

James, W. (2007). *The principles of psychology* (Vol. 1). Cosimo, Inc.

Kashdan, T. B., Disabato, D. J., Goodman, F. R., & Naughton, C. (2018). The five dimensions of curiosity. *Harvard Business Review, 96*(5), 58–60.

Kashdan, T. B., Goodman, F. R., Disabato, D. J., McKnight, P. E., Kelso, K., & Naughton, C. (2020a). Curiosity has comprehensive benefits in the workplace: Developing and validating a multidimensional workplace curiosity scale in United States and German employees. *Personality and Individual Differences, 155*, (1), 109717.

Kashdan, T. B., Stiksma, M. C., Disabato, D. J., McKnight, P. E., Bekier, J., Kaji, J., & Lazarus, R. (2020b). The five-dimensional curiosity scale: Capturing the bandwidth of curiosity and identifying four unique subgroups of curious people. *Journal of Research in Personality, 73*, 130–149.

Lewis, M. (2003). *Moneyball: The art of winning an unfair game.* W.W. Norton & Company.

Lewis, M. (2010). *The big short: Inside the doomsday machine.* W.W. Norton & Company.

Lewis, M. (2018). *The fifth risk.* W.W. Norton & Company.

Lewis, M. (2021). *The premonition: A pandemic story.* W.W. Norton & Company.

Litman, J. A., & Spielberger, C. D. (2003). Measuring epistemic curiosity and its diversive and specific components. *Journal of Personality Assessment, 80*(1), 75–86.

Loewenstein, G. (1994). The psychology of curiosity: A review and reinterpretation. *Psychological Bulletin, 116*(1), 75–98.

Manson, N. C. (2012). Epistemic restraint and the vice of curiosity. *Philosophy, 87*(340), 239–259.

McDonald III, B. D. (2010). The Bureau of Municipal research and the development of a professional public service. *Administration & Society, 42*(7), 815–835.

Murray, N., Sujan, H., Hirt, E. R., & Sujan, M. (1990). The influence of mood on categorization: A cognitive flexibility interpretation. *Journal of Personality and Social Psychology, 59*(3), 411–425.

Opdal, P. M. (2001). Curiosity, wonder and education seen as perspective development. *Studies in Philosophy and Education, 20*(4), 331–344.

Phillips, R. (2016). Curious about others: Relational and empathetic curiosity for diverse societies. *New Formations: A Journal of Culture/Theory/Politics, 88*(88), 123–142.

Pluck, G., & Johnson, H. L. (2011). Stimulating curiosity to enhance learning. *GESJ: Education Sciences and Psychology, 2*(19), 1512–1801.

Robertson, D. J. (2012). New voices: The curious case of Sherlock Holmes and perceptual load. *The Psychologist, 25*, 472–475.

Rossing, B. E., & Long, H. B. (1981). Contributions of curiosity and relevance to adult learning motivation. *Adult Education, 32*(1), 25–36.

Sansone, C., & Thoman, D. B. (2005). Interest as the missing motivator in self-regulation. *European Psychologist, 10*(3), 175–186.

Schmitt, F. F., & Lahroodi, R. (2008). The epistemic value of curiosity. *Educational Theory, 58*(2), 125–148.

Silvia, P. J. (2005). What is interesting? Exploring the appraisal structure of interest. *Emotion, 5*, 89–102.

Silvia, P. J. (2006). *Exploring the psychology of interest.* Oxford University Press.

Silvia, P. J. (2008). Interest – the curious emotion. *Current Directions in Psychological Science, 17*(1), 57–60.

Stagl, J. (1995). *A history of curiosity: The theory of travel, 1550–1800* (Vol. 13). Psychology Press.

Walsh, P. G. (1988). The rights and wrongs of curiosity (Plutarch to Augustine). *Greece & Rome, 35*(1), 73–85.

Zurn, P. (2021). *Curiosity and power: The politics of inquiry.* University of Minnesota Press.

3 Theoretical Framework of the Curious Public Administrator

The last decade showed that public administration is at crossroads in the U.S. One route will go down the path of continuation with public administrators serving as functionaries while democratic governance in the U.S. weakens beyond the point of rebuilding its institutions. The other hopeful path is one where public administration plays a vital role in building a nation with empathetic, caring, fair, and democratic institutions to help fight for social equity and empowerment for all its citizens. But to pick this route, public administration needs a new guiding framework or doctrine. A few years ago, I wrote an essay for *Public Integrity* (2019) sketching the outline of this doctrine (Hatcher, 2019). As I discussed in that essay and recounted in Chapter 1 of this book, public administrators driven by curiosity, or the desire to practice empathy to question how the world works and make decisions rooted in evidence, could benefit the public service through fostering public participation, demonstrating caring, and rebuilding the public's trust in government. To accomplish this, we must construct a theoretical framework for curiosity in public administration settings.

Chapters 1 and 2 laid the foundation for this framework by introducing curiosity, defining the concept, and aligning that definition in the scholarly literature. Next, we build on this foundation by discussing related research in public administration and identifying concepts to craft a theoretical framework. We will use the framework to develop propositions of how the concepts in the framework relate to one another to test, define, and refine the doctrine of the curious public administrator (Bacharach, 1989). To organize the framework, we will conceptualize curiosity, discuss key variables from research, and discuss previous theories and ideas in public administration.

Conceptualization

Referencing the definition of curiosity formed in the previous chapters, *Curiosity is the intellectual motivation to learn objectively how the world works*; the following key concepts can be identified: motivation, objectivity, and empirical

DOI: 10.4324/9781032668826-3

knowledge (i.e., how the world works). Chapter 1 seeks to do this by unpacking the definition of curiosity. The following sections extend these concepts to develop the book's theoretical framework.

Motivation

This book's approach to curiosity assumes that the concept is an intrinsic motivation of employees. There is a rich literature on what motivates individuals in organizations and public administration (Vandenabeele et al., 2014). The findings from this literature can inform this study on curiosity. PSM explains how different values drive public servants than their private sector counterparts, mainly focusing on the public good. Through this motivation, public administrators practice empathy for others by being concerned about the community at the expense of individual motivators. In her analysis of the Housing Authority of the City of Baltimore, Dolamore (2021) tested a framework to identify an organizational culture of empathy in public agencies. This framework included policies, socialization, leadership behavior, rewards and recognition, discourse in the organization, learning, and other factors that focus on promoting empathy and understanding throughout an organization. And empathy in an organization includes a focus on the needs of individuals, such as the residents of the Housing Authority in City of Baltimore in the study by Dolamore (2021). The framework of empathy in public organizations has a connected theme in many ways, public servants being motivated by curiosity and caring.

And by motivating care for others, curiosity promotes care organizations and compassionate organizations. However, some of the literature studies on organizational behavior view caring and compassion as a conflict with resources and in the private sector earning money in an organization (Peus, 2011). In other words, caring often is viewed at odds with performance-focused organizations or what may be described as "masculine rationality" (Saks, 2021). However, the motivations in the public sector can push public service-orientated organizations and fields, such as nursing, social work, and community development, toward caring and compassion in organizational behavior. And managers in all settings should be able to use the tools of motivation through curiosity to build caring organizations. By caring organizations, I mean ones described by Fuqua and Newman (2002) as having the following characteristics: gratitude, forgiveness, encouragement, compassion, community, sensitivity, tolerance, charity, and inclusion. And as Tronto (2010) argued, organizations encourage "pluralistic, particular tailoring of care to meet individuals' needs" (p. 158). Caring organizations are ones where managers and other members are motivated by the elements discussed by Fuqua and Newman (2002), focusing on what Tronto (2010) notes as the diverse needs of individuals in the organization.

Objectivity

The book approaches objectivity from the standpoint of a public servant seeking to understand how the world works. Thus, there is a need to collect "truths" of the world. Moreover, objectivity in public organizations is concerned with exploring the truth and providing transparency to the public (Nelson, 2002). Public administrators typically are more concerned with objectivity and have a higher standard of the concept in practice than elective officials (Mulgan, 2007).

However, the definition of objectivity is highly debated in public administration. For instance, Hummel (1991) argued that public administrators do not make decisions using objectivity and rationality, but individuals working in organizations build their realities through "story-telling." And there is value in collecting these stories as rich data sources to help researchers explain and describe how public administrators do their jobs and how public organizations function. Furthermore, more post-modernist critiques of objectivity have successfully demonstrated that reality is often subjective in nature (Dworkin, 1996). For our theory of curious public administration, we need to move beyond the traditional dichotomy of objectivity and subjectivity toward understanding how public administrators gather information and use that knowledge to make effective decisions—whether through heavily quantitative analysis or storytelling (Raadschelders, 2011). Both tools can help curious administrators collect knowledge.

Empirical Knowledge

Learning through study and experience are critical components of curiosity. To help us build a theoretical description of interest in public administration that does not get bogged down in debates over objectivity versus subjectivity, we need a framework that focuses on gathering knowledge of the world for organizations to make decisions. To do this, we can use the concept of "learning organizations." What is a learning organization? Senge (2006) described learning organizations as encouraging the search for information that can help achieve goals, even when that information may be initially negative for leadership and others in the organization. This type of learning in organizations goes hand in hand with curiosity. And public administration, even in highly legalistic areas such as criminal justice, has been able to put in place learning organizations, with some costs but often more benefits (Brown & Brudney, 2003).

Centering the Theory of Curiosity in Public Administration Scholarship

The following section details theories in public administration or ones that have been applied to public administration from other fields to identify aspects that may be useful to construct the book's theoretical framework of a curious public administrator. This section discusses theories useful to building the book's framework for curiosity in public administration. To do this, we need to trace curiosity through the early years of the evolution of public administration as a scholarly discipline, starting with Max Weber, who is often labeled as the Father of Modern Bureaucracy. While Weber did not discuss curiosity specifically in his writings about administration and bureaucracy, the author did discuss the concept regarding the individual level in organizations. In *Science as Vocation*, Weber (Åkerström, 2013) described curiosity as needing to be kept through "strange intoxication" for the work that one performs (p. 10). While not a scholar, Frederick Taylor is often included in the early years of public administration as a scholarly discipline as a proponent of professional management and efficiency through Scientific Management (Waring, 2016; Frederickson et al., 2018.) The Scientific Management approach seeks to identify the "one best way" or most efficient act to perform administrative tasks. In doing so, there is a hint of curiosity, but not in the same manner as described in this book, which includes a focus on curiosity to expand beyond a single-minded focus on efficiency to other areas critical to administration, such as effectiveness, fairness, equity, and democratic values.

Scientific Management's primary focus is on efficiency, and the one best way puts forth a machine impression of administration. The ideas of Mary Parker Follett called for public administration to focus on the human side of administration (Feldheim, 2003; Newman & Guy, 1998). By focusing on the needs and motivations of the people in organizations, public administrators (and researchers studying them) need to practice curiosity to solve problems. Herbert Simon's ideas of bounded rationality extended this focus on individuals making decisions and the curiosity of looking for not the one best way (i.e., maximizing) but the best solution among the available options (i.e., satisficing) (Frederickson et al., 2018).

After World War II, the public administration theory branched into multiple directions or steams. The work by Dwight Waldo and then H. George Frederickson promotes the importance of values and equity in the practice and study of public administration (Bryer & Cooper, 2012). Following this New Public Administration focus, curiosity can be considered vital in understanding, explaining, and advocating the role of values, equity, and democratic governance in public organizations. Conversely, the ideas of New Public Management and its focus on efficiency return the field and this discussion on curiosity back to a narrow, single-minded view. The field has moved beyond this view. Today, public administration focuses on multiple viewpoints. The field's top theories involve ensuring social equity, incorporating technology, understanding networks in policymaking and implementation, promoting democratic governance, and other intellectual ideas beyond efficiency. Curiosity in public administration is the next step in this theoretical journey.

The arguments that Roberts (2020) puts forth in *Strategies for Governing* can help us center the theory of curiosity in public administration scholarship—in particular, his focus on the future of public administration through the lens of macro-level, meso-level, and micro-level analyses (p. 17). The theory of administrative curiosity has individual, intermediate, and macro-level features. We use these lenses to examine individuals, organizations, and the overall view of public administration faculty on curiosity.

Constructing a Theoretical Framework

This chapter and the previous two have presented conceptual ideas of curiosity and its virtue for public organizations and their administrators. But before we can examine these ideas in practice, a theoretical framework connecting the ideas needs to be constructed. Thus, based on the theories and research reviewed in this book so far, the following curious public administrators demonstrate the following work-related features:

- First, they are knowledge seekers and are intrinsically motivated to find it.
- Second, they practice empathy in the workplace.
- Third, seeking knowledge and practicing empathy help curious administrators care about their colleagues and the people they serve.
- Lastly, seeking knowledge, practicing empathy, and caring lead curious administrators to be better learners than managers who lack curiosity, leading to learning and adaptive public organizations.

Accordingly, these factors can be used to construct hypotheses that will be tested in the remaining chapters of this book. The hypotheses will be tested at the individual level by examining survey data collected from city managers. The hypotheses will be tested at the organizational level by profiling public organizations that demonstrate the factors of curiosity discussed in this chapter. Lastly, a set of guiding research questions is constructed to examine what public affairs faculty think about these factors of curiosity and how they teach current and future public managers the concepts.

Individual-Level Hypotheses

The following are guiding research questions and hypotheses that will be used to examine individual-level curiosity in public employees, in particular city managers.

Hypothesis 1: Curious public administrators are more likely to view the objective search for knowledge as a crucial part of their jobs than other parts of their work. This can be examined by the Joyous Exploration,

Deprivation Sensitivity, and Stress Tolerance parts of the Workplace Curiosity Scale.

Hypothesis 2: Curious public administrators are more likely to express the importance of practicing empathy as a part of their jobs, compared to other parts of their work. This can be examined by the Openness to People's Ideas part of the Workplace Curiosity Scale.

Hypothesis 3: Curious public administrators are more likely to express the importance of demonstrating caring behaviors as part of their jobs, compared to other parts of their work. This can be examined by questions developed for this study on the relationship between caring and curiosity in the public workplace.

Hypothesis 4: Curious public administrators are more likely to express the importance of learning, not just searching for knowledge, as part of their jobs, compared to other parts of their work. This can be examined by all parts of the study's survey and the Workplace Curiosity Scale.

In the following chapter, survey questions examining these hypotheses will be constructed. The results of those survey questions will be compared to the respondent's answers on the curiosity instrument used from the literature. The Workplace Curiosity Scale developed by Kashdan et al. (2020) is a critical component of the individual-level survey. The overall survey is discussed in greater detail in Chapter 4 of this book.

Public Affairs Faculty and Curiosity

The book lastly examines how public affairs faculty view curiosity and teach it in their classrooms. Instead of being guided by hypotheses, this section will be guided by the following research questions.

What do public affairs faculty think about the features of curiosity?
What do public affairs faculty think about the importance of the features of curiosity compared to other areas of information?
How do public affairs faculty define curiosity?
How do public affairs faculty teach curiosity in their classrooms?
Are there differences between the faculty who view curiosity as vital and those who do not see it as important?

Organizational-Level Hypotheses

The book also examines how curiosity affects overall public organizations. This part of the research is meant to show how the actions of curious public managers can influence a public organization. To understand the features of curious public organizations, a collection of public agencies demonstrating the factors of curiosity will be identified and analyzed using the following guiding hypothesis.

Hypothesis 1: Curious public organizations demonstrate adaptive learning
Hypothesis 2: Curious public organizations demonstrate empathy.
Hypothesis 3: Curious public organizations demonstrate caring.

We can also examine the failures of leaders and organizations that do not practice curiosity. For instance, the Centers for Disease Control and Prevention during the early days of the COVID-19 pandemic allowed politics to overrun curiosity, and the actions of President Trump during this time demonstrate a leader motivated more by self-preservation than curiosity. By conducting these analyses of three levels, inspired by the approach taken by Roberts (2020), we can examine questions and hypotheses of how curiosity affects public managers and their work, how curiosity affects overall organizations, and how academics in public administration view curiosity as a concept in the classroom.

References

Åkerström, M. (2013). Curiosity and serendipity in qualitative research. *Qualitative Sociology Review, 9*(2), 10–18.

Bacharach, S. B. (1989). Organizational theories: Some criteria for evaluation. *Academy of Management Review, 14*(4), 496–515.

Brown, M. M., & Brudney, J. L. (2003). Learning organizations in the public sector? A study of police agencies employing information and technology to advance knowledge. *Public Administration Review, 63*(1), 30–43.

Bryer, T. A., & Cooper, T. L. (2012). H. George Frederickson and the dialogue on citizenship in public administration. *Public Administration Review, 72*(s1), S108–S116.

Dolamore, S. (2021). Detecting empathy in public organizations: Creating a more relational public administration. *Administrative Theory & Praxis, 43*(1), 58–81.

Dworkin, R. (1996). Objectivity and truth: You'd better believe it. *Philosophy & Public Affairs, 25*(2), 87–139.

Feldheim, M. A. (2003). Mary Parker Follett lost and found-again, and again, and again. *International Journal of Organization Theory & Behavior, 7*(3), 341–362.

Frederickson, H. G., Smith, K. B., Larimer, C. W., & Licari, M. J. (2018). *The public administration theory primer*. Routledge.

Fuqua, D. R., & Newman, J. L. (2002). Creating caring organizations. *Consulting Psychology Journal: Practice and Research, 54*(2), 131.

Hatcher, W. (2019). The curious public administrator: The new administrative doctrine. *Public Integrity, 21*(3), 225–228.

Hummel, R. P. (1991). Stories managers tell: Why they are as valid as science. *Public Administration Review, 31*(1), 31–41.

Kashdan, T. B., Goodman, F. R., Disabato, D. J., McKnight, P. E., Kelso, K., & Naughton, C. (2020). Curiosity has comprehensive benefits in the workplace: Developing and validating a multidimensional workplace curiosity scale in United States and German employees. *Personality and Individual Differences, 155*, 109717.

Mulgan, R. (2007). Truth in government and the politicization of public service advice. *Public Administration, 85*(3), 569–586.

Nelson, L. (2002). Protecting the common good: Technology, objectivity, and privacy. *Public Administration Review, 62*, 69–73.

Newman, M. A., & Guy, M. E. (1998). Taylor's triangle, Follett's web. *Administrative Theory & Praxis, (20)*3, 287–297.

Peus, C. (2011). Money over man versus caring and compassion? Challenges for today's organizations and their leaders. *Journal of Organizational Behavior, 32*(7), 955–960.

Raadschelders, J. C. (2011). The future of the study of public administration: Embedding research object and methodology in epistemology and ontology. *Public Administration Review, 71*(6), 916–924.

Roberts, A. (2020). *Strategies for governing.* Cornell University Press.

Saks, A. M. (2021). A model of caring in organizations for human resource development. *Human Resource Development Review*, 15344843211024035.

Senge, P. M. (2006). *The fifth discipline: The art and practice of the learning organization.* Currency.

Tronto, J. C. (2010). Creating caring institutions: Politics, plurality, and purpose. *Ethics and Social Welfare, 4*(2), 158–171.

Vandenabeele, W., Brewer, G. A., & Ritz, A. (2014). Past, present, and future of public service motivation research. *Public Administration, 92*(4), 779–789.

Waring, S. P. (2016). *Taylorism transformed: Scientific management theory since 1945.* UNC Press Books.

4 Curious Public Administrators

So far, this book has defined curiosity, discussed past academic literature and studies on the concept, and aligned the concept with the public administration literature. In Chapter 3, I constructed a framework of the curious public administrator based on the literature reviewed in Chapters 1 and 2. To examine the framework along with its hypotheses and research assumptions, I administered two surveys for this book: a survey to the chief administrative officers of U.S. cities to find out what they think about curiosity and another survey to the public administration faculty working for NASPAA programs. Municipal managers were surveyed to gather data on how practitioners throughout the nation view curiosity. In particular, the survey collects data on how public administrators approach curiosity by administering a standardized index validated in the literature (Kashdan et al., 2020) and how they view the concept affecting their work. The survey of faculty working in NASPAA member institutions also has a twofold goal to collect data on how they view curiosity in their professional lives and to gain knowledge on how they approach the concept in public affairs curricula and classrooms. In Chapter 4, I detail the survey to municipal managers and discuss the overall findings.

I administered two surveys for this research: one survey of the chief administrative officers to find out what they think about curiosity and another survey of public administration faculty working for NASPAA programs. This chapter reports and discusses the findings from the survey to local public administrators in U.S. cities.

Local Government Managers and Curiosity

As noted in earlier chapters of this book, the literature on curiosity in public administration needs to be expanded. It often focuses on the importance of other values and concepts, such as empathy (Dolamore, 2021). Thus, as stressed, this chapter aims to expand the curiosity literature on public administration by surveying an essential group of public administrators, the chief administrative officers of U.S. cities. The research on local government management and city managers/administrators is extensive, focusing on gender disparities (Alexander,

DOI: 10.4324/9781032668826-4

2015; Alkadry et al., 2019; Beaty & Davis, 2012), tenure and turnover of managers (Ammons & Bosse, 2005), career paths (Hatcher et al., 2022; Watson & Hassett, 2003, 2004), and structures of local government (Frederickson et al., 2004). So far, the literature on local government management has yet to focus on curiosity and its effect on the jobs of these public servants.

For instance, a search of *Public Administration Review*, arguably the field's flagship journal, found zero empirical studies focused explicitly on curiosity and public administration. From the search, though, I found an interesting commentary by Donald Stone from 1981. In his essay, Stone argued that innovative organizations need managers who are also innovative. And he stressed that innovation comes from "sustained curiosity." He continues to make this argument for the relationship between curiosity and innovation in administration by citing Louis Brownlow's stance that "the principal requirement of a good administrator is an insatiable curiosity" (Stone, 1981, p. 507).

As noted throughout this book, I searched public administration literature broadly. I found few studies specifically on curiosity in public administration and, for the purposes of this chapter, local government management and curiosity. However, scholars have examined the intersections of creativity and local government management. Kruyen and van Genugten (2017) interviewed civil servants about the efficacy of creativity in public administration, particularly local government management. The authors applied the business literature's view of creativity—that is, that the concept drives managers toward finding new ideas—and found that the civil servants viewed the concept as necessary in their work but did not see it as the dominant factor leading to innovation in administration.

Given the lack of previous studies on curiosity and local government management, what can we use to help build the theoretical foundations of the analysis reporting in this chapter? The literature on PSM and city management can help advance this chapter's review of scholarship. The PSM survey instruments (Perry, 1997; Ritz et al., 2016) contain questions focusing on what drives public servants to do their jobs; such motivating factors as extrinsic rewards and intrinsic variables are included. The survey statements include references to empathy, the desire to make a difference, a focus on the public good, and other values closely related to this book's view of curiosity in public administration.

Another stream of literature that can help advance this chapter's focus on curiosity and city management is the collection of research focusing on organizational learning. The case made in this book with the theory of administrative curiosity is that public administrators are most effective, efficient, and fair when they ask questions about the world and genuinely care about finding the answers to those questions. At its foundation, this is a process of learning, and public administrators are parts of organizations, so it is a process of organizational learning sparked by individual curiosity in daily aspects of work. What has past research taught us about organizational learning? It combines structural (rules in organizations) and cultural factors

(Moynihan & Landuyt, 2009). Writing in *Public Administration Review*, Moynihan and Landuyt (2009) present a strong argument for "learning forums," where organizational learning is driven by workgroups focused on specific tasks that allow for multiple viewpoints, including dissenting opinions. These learning forums can be viewed through the lens of this book's theory of administrative curiosity as groups of public administrators practice curiosity in tackling an organizational problem objectively and empirically to learn how the world works. Thus, public bureaucracies strongly committed to learning forums can be viewed as curious organizations.

The last stream of literature that can inform this chapter's examination of administrative curiosity in city management is the research on curiosity in the workplace. This research has already been mentioned in the book in building the literature behind the theory of administrative curiosity. As noted, the research focuses primarily on the private sector. The research conducted for this chapter uses a specific survey instrument from the curiosity workplace literature developed by Kashdan et al. (2020) to assess individuals' curiosity in the workplace.

Surveying City Managers/Administrators

To examine this curiosity in local government management, I constructed a survey instrument to collect data on chief administrative officers' viewpoints regarding curiosity as a concept for public administration practice. The survey has 29 questions that collected data in the following areas: characteristics of the cities where the managers work, the demographics of the managers, and their educational backgrounds. Next, the survey includes a 16-question instrument assessing the curiosity levels of the local public managers in the study. The instrument is a standardized and validated survey from the research literature on curiosity. Kashdan et al. (2019) developed the instrument to assess the multiple dimensions of curiosity in the workplace. The authors titled the instrument the M-Workplace Curiosity Scale. The instrument is rooted in the literature on curiosity, but as the authors write, as of 2019, "there is no research on how multiple dimensions of curiosity operate in the workplace" (p. 1). This chapter's survey expands the research to the public sector workplace by asking local public managers to complete the M-Workplace Curiosity Scale.

I administered the survey to the chief administrative offices in U.S. cities with populations greater than 10,000. These are the public managers in the U.S. who significantly influence the day-to-day lives of the public and their communities. By collecting data from cities between 10,000 and 50,000 residents, the results of this survey present information on an important topic, curiosity in public administration, from a typically understudied group, local public managers working in small- to medium-sized cities. These communities are often overlooked in the research, with many studies surveying and studying cities with more than 50,000 or 25,000 residents. In their book *Managing America's Small Communities*, Folz and French (2005) make an excellent case for studying public administration in small localities because most of America, while still urban, comprises individuals living in these communities. Moreover, professional local managers lead many of these municipalities. Most cities in the U.S. have populations between 10,000 and 50,000 residents, many of which are council-manager systems of local government (ICMA, 2015; NLC, N/D).

The survey was administered using an email database of the chief administrative officers of cities with populations over 10,000. The cities were identified using the 2018 American Community Survey's five-year estimates. The websites of these cities were reviewed to identify the chief administrative officers and to locate their contact email addresses. Following these steps and after removing email addresses that were no longer active, a database of 1,980 municipalities was constructed. This database represents the survey's sample, and the sampling frame is the 1,980 chief administrative officers of these communities. The survey was administrated via Qualtrics through emails in multiple waves between June 28, 2022 and July 28, 2022. From these survey waves, 192 local public administrators completed the survey. Eight of these individuals were identified as mayors, and other officials were not in chief administrative officer positions. These respondents did not complete the entire survey. Accordingly, 9% of the surveyed local public administrators completed the survey.

The Study's City Managers

Given the variety of local government forms in the U.S., I defined chief administrative officers as city managers and city administrators. In some small communities, the day-to-day local public manager is the city clerk. Given these various forms of local chief administrative officers, the survey asked respondents to identify their position and their city's form of local government.

While the response rate for the survey was low, the sample appeared to be representative of the broad population of local public managers working in U.S. municipalities. Most of the respondents were identified as city managers (61%), which aligns with the fact that many small- to medium-sized cities have manager-council forms of local government. For instance, 81% of the survey's respondents reported working in a council-manager form of municipal government. However, a large percentage of the local managers surveyed were identified as city administrators (27%), which may be indicative of a trend that the "adaptive city" structure has become more prevalent throughout the nation (Frederickson et al., 2004). Small percentages of respondents were identified as city clerks (4%) or other titles (7%), such as directors of administrative services. Most respondents were identified as working in cities in the Midwest (40%) and the South (35%). As noted, most municipalities in the U.S. have populations below 25,000 people. Thus, it is no surprise that most of the respondents (47%) work in cities of this size.

The demographics of the survey's sample reflect how local government management is still not diverse and often not representative of the communities served (Beaty & Davis, 2012; Fox & Schuhmann, 1999; Kellogg et al., 2019; Holman, 2017; Alkadry et al., 2019). Seventy-six percent of the samples were identified as men, whereas 25% were identified as women. This percentage approximates the results in the published literature (Feeney & Camarena, 2019). Most of the surveyed municipal public administrators (72%) reported being between 45 and 64 years old. Most startlingly is the lack of racial diversity among the municipal public administrators, with 95% of the sample being identified as white. This is also similar to what has been reported in other similar surveys in the peer-reviewed literature (Feeney & Camarena, 2019). Researchers have written about the need to study the lack of diversity in local government management in more detail, but unfortunately, few empirical studies have been implemented, and even fewer analyses of small- to medium-sized cities (Feeney & Camarena, 2021).

Lastly, an interesting finding in the descriptive data of the sample's characteristics is how a majority of the municipal public administrators (56%) hold Master of Public Administration (MPA) degrees, indicating the viability of that degree as a career path to the profession of local government management. The sample in this chapter's survey reflects the population of city managers as described earlier and in Tables 4.1 and 4.2 as detailed by recent research (Hatcher

Table 4.1 Characteristics and Demographics of the Study's Sample of Chief Administrative Officers

Category	Variable	N	Valid %
Position Type (N = 175)	City Manager	107	61.14
	City Administrator	48	27.43
	City Clear	7	4.00
	Other	13	7.43
Region (N = 173)	Northeast	7	4.05
	South	61	35.26
	Midwest	69	39.88
	West	36	20.81
Form of Government (N = 173)	Mayor-Council	33	19.08
	Council-Manager	140	80.92
City's Population (N = 173)	Over 1 million	1	0.6
	500,000–1 million	1	0.6
	250,000–499,999	0	0.0
	100,000–249,999	15	8.67
	50,000–99, 999	36	20.81
	25,000–49,999	39	22.54
	Less than 25,000	81	46.82
Gender (N = 173)	Female	42	24.28
	Male	131	75.72
Age (N = 172)	25–34	3	1.74
	35–44	25	14.53
	45–54	61	35.47
	55–64	63	36.63
	65 and older	19	11.05

Race (N = 170)	American Indian or Alaska Native	0	0.0
	Asian	1	0.6
	Black or African American	0	0.0
	White	7	4.12
		162	95.29
Education (N = 173)	No college degree	3	1.73
	Bachelor's Degree	32	18.50
	Master of Public Administration	96	55.49
	Master of Business Administration	16	9.25
	Other type of master's degree	26	15.03

Source: Created by the author

Note: Based on the U.S. Census, the states in each region are as follows: **Northeast** = Connecticut, Maine, Massachusetts, New Hampshire, New Jersey, New York, Pennsylvania, Rhode Island, and Vermont; **South** = Alabama, Arkansas, Delaware, District of Columbia, Florida, Georgia, Kentucky, Louisiana, Maryland, Mississippi, North Carolina, Oklahoma, South Carolina, Tennessee, Texas, Virginia, and West Virginia; **Midwest** = Illinois, Indiana, Iowa, Kansas, Michigan, Minnesota, Missouri, Nebraska, North Dakota, Ohio, South Dakota, and Wisconsin; **West** = Alaska, Arizona, California, Colorado, Hawaii, Idaho, Montana, Nevada, New Mexico, Oregon, Washington, and Wyoming. The form of government variable is based on the International City/County Management Association's (ICMA) definitions, which are as follows: **Mayor-Council** = Elected council or board serves as the legislative body. The chief elected official is the head of government, with significant administrative authority, generally elected separately from the council; **Council-Manager** = Elected council or board and chief elected official (e.g., mayor) are responsible for making policy with advice of the chief appointed official. A professional administrator appointed by the board or council has full responsibility for the day-to-day operation of the government. **Commission** = Members of a board of elected commissioners serve as head of specific departments and collectively sit as the legislative body of government.

Table 4.2 Comparison of Survey Respondents With U.S. Municipalities

	Number of Respondents	Percent of Respondents	Percent of U.S. Municipalities (10,000 or Greater)
Over 1,000,000	1	0.6	0.3
500,000–1,000,000	1	0.6	0.9
250,000–499,999	0	0.0	1.7
100,000–249,999	15	8.67	7.3
50,000–99,999	36	20.81	15.1
25,000–49,999	39	22.54	24.0
10,000–24,999	81	46.82	50.8
Northeast	7	4.05	14.6
South	61	35.26	36.3
Midwest	69	39.88	24.6
West	36	20.81	24.5

Source: Created by the author

Note: U.S. municipalities calculated as a percentage of all municipalities over 10,000.

et al., 2022) and available Census data. In the following sections, I discuss how these samples view curiosity and how the concept influences their behavior in their public workplaces.

Curiosity Among City Managers

The survey administered a series of questions to the sampled city managers seeking to assess their viewpoints on their approach to curiosity and work and the overall concept of curiosity in the workplace. To do this, I relied on the validated instrument for the studies on curiosity in the workplace of private companies (Kashdan et al., 2019), and in doing so, I applied it to the workplace of public organizations for the first time. The following analyses found that city managers are highly curious in their approach to their work, and there are specific themes of groupings among the surveyed public administrators.

Not surprisingly, public administrators reported levels of curiosity through their answers on the Kashdan et al. (2019) instrument. The instrument is comprised of 16 statements of curiosity. These statements are detailed in Table 4.3. The instrument asks respondents to provide their opinions on these

Table 4.3 Curiosity in the Public Workplace: City Managers

#	Statements	Minimum	Maximum	Mean	Std. Deviation	Variance	Count
1	I enjoy that I often find my mind continues to work through complex problems outside of work.	1.00	5.00	3.89	0.78	0.62	161
2	I get excited thinking about experimenting with different ideas.	2.00	5.00	4.01	0.76	0.57	161
3	At work, I seek out opportunities to expand my knowledge or skills.	2.00	5.00	4.14	0.69	0.47	160
4	I seek out work tasks where I will have to think in-depth about something.	1.00	5.00	3.88	0.80	0.64	161
5	When given a complex problem at work, I can't rest until I find the answer.	1.00	5.00	3.60	0.85	0.73	160
6	When a complex work problem arises, I continue to seek information until I understand it fully.	2.00	5.00	4.01	0.76	0.58	160

7	I can spend hours on a single problem because I feel a need to find an answer.	1.00	5.00	3.03	0.98	0.96	159
8	I work relentlessly to find answers to complicated questions at work.	1.00	5.00	3.41	0.90	0.80	160
9	When work is anxiety provoking, I tend to explore rather than avoid.	1.00	5.00	3.53	0.90	0.81	161
10	The possibility of being distressed does not impact my motivation to work on new projects.	1.00	5.00	3.64	0.99	0.98	160
11	I do not shy away from the unknown or unfamiliar even if it seems scary.	2.00	5.00	4.09	0.85	0.73	161
12	When probing deeper into a project that interests me, feeling anxious does not derail me.	1.00	5.00	3.98	0.84	0.71	161
13	It is important to listen to ideas from people who think differently.	3.00	5.00	4.49	0.65	0.42	161
14	I value colleagues with different ideas.	3.00	5.00	4.51	0.56	0.31	160
15	I like to hear ideas from colleagues even if they are different from my current line of thinking.	2.00	5.00	4.47	0.62	0.39	161
16	Even when I am confident in my approach to a problem, I like to hear other people's opinions.	2.00	5.00	4.29	0.67	0.44	161

Source: Created by the author

Note: Here are statements people often use to describe themselves. Thinking of your job and your workplace, please indicate the degree to which each statement has been characteristic of you. There are no right or wrong answers—ranging from very slightly or not at all (1) to extremely (5).

statements considering their jobs and workplaces. Their answers can range from "very slightly or not all (1) to extremely (5)." Kashdan et al. (2019) organized, using factor analysis, the answers of private sector managers to the statements into four groups: Joyous Exploration (statements 1–4), Deprivation Sensitivity (statements 5–8), Stress Tolerance (statements 9–12), and Openness to People's Ideas (statements 13–16).

Table 4.3 reports the answers of surveyed public administrators on the 16 statements. Most of the respondents (161) completed this part of the survey. As can be seen by the mean values, the public administrators surveyed value curiosity in the workplace. The respondents mainly found themselves curious in the following areas: valuing colleagues with different ideas, listening to people who think differently, hearing ideas different from their current thinking, and listening to others even when they are confident with their opinion. While still supportive of curiosity, respondents were less curious when it came to the following: spending hours on a single problem, working restlessly until they found an answer, and resting while faced with a complex problem.

To understand the differences of opinion on curiosity in the workplace among the surveyed public administrators, I conducted a factor analysis of their answers on the 16 statements instrument. Table 4.4 details the factor

Table 4.4 Curiosity in the Public Workplace: Factor Analysis

	Component			
	1	2	3	4
I enjoy that I often find my mind continues to work through complex problems outside of work.	.463	.107	.323	.412
I get excited thinking about experimenting with different ideas.	.506	.207	.113	.570
At work, I seek out opportunities to expand my knowledge or skills.	.570	.018	.198	.249
I seek out work tasks where I will have to think in-depth about something.	.564	.123	.162	.507
When given a complex problem at work, I can't rest until I find the answer.	.515	.443	.274	−.278
When a complex work problem arises, I continue to seek information until I understand it fully.	.533	.404	.253	−.305
I can spend hours on a single problem because I feel a need to find an answer.	.515	.470	.213	−.390
I work relentlessly to find answers to complicated questions at work.	.662	.446	.050	−.129
When work is anxiety provoking, I tend to explore rather than avoid.	.601	.129	−.090	−.146
The possibility of being distressed does not impact my motivation to work on new projects.	.650	.121	−.573	.048
I do not shy away from the unknown or unfamiliar even if it seems scary.	.706	.058	−.485	−.006

When probing deeper into a project that interests me, feeling anxious does not derail me.	.605	.008	−.624	.019
It is important to listen to ideas from people who think differently.	.598	−.562	.217	−.196
I value colleagues with different ideas.	.597	−.637	.129	−.087
I like to hear ideas from colleagues even if they are different from my current line of thinking.	.647	−.634	.154	−.040
Even when I am confident in my approach to a problem, I like to hear other people's opinions.	.507	−.575	.019	−.139

Source: Created by the author

Note: Here are statements people often use to describe themselves. Thinking of your job and your workplace, please indicate the degree to which each statement has been characteristic of you. There are no right or wrong answers—ranging from very slightly or not at all (1) to extremely (5). Significant loadings of 0.50 or higher are highlighted.

analysis results, showing the loadings of four groups. Each of these groups had Eigenvalues of 1.0 or higher, indicating a significant dimension of opinion. Group 1 had an Eigenvalue of 5.403. Group 2 had an Eigenvalue of 2.337. Group 3 had an Eigenvalue of 1.417. And lastly, Group 4 had an Eigenvalue of 1.244. Examining the factor loading for each question in these groups can help us identify meaningful themes throughout the data. A loading of 0.50 or higher is significant and indicates a distinct opinion on that statement. Group 1 contains loadings of 0.50 or higher on all the statements except the first one, which at 0.436 is close to 0.50. Given the loading on all but one statement, this group can be considered the most curious. Group 2 shows an interesting loading of negative values on the last four statements that specifically address practicing curiosity with others. They may not value differences from others in their curiosity about the world as much as the others in the sample. Groups 3 and 4 have few significant loadings, and both lack a coherent theme in their grouping.

- **Hypothesis 1:** Curious public administrators are more likely to view the objective search for knowledge as a crucial part of their jobs than other parts of their work. This can be examined by the Joyous Exploration, Deprivation Sensitivity, and Stress Tolerance parts of the Workplace Curiosity Scale.
- **Hypothesis 2:** Curious public administrators are more likely to express the importance of practicing empathy as a part of their jobs, compared to other parts of their work. This can be examined by the Openness to People's Ideas part of the Workplace Curiosity Scale.
- **Hypothesis 3:** Curious public administrators are more likely to express the importance of demonstrating caring behaviors as part of their jobs, compared to other parts of their work. This can be examined by questions developed for this study on the relationship between caring and curiosity in the public workplace.

- **Hypothesis 4:** Curious public administrators are more likely to express the importance of learning, not just searching for knowledge, as part of their jobs, compared to other parts of their work. This can be examined by all parts of the study's survey and the M-Workplace Curiosity Scale.

To recap and compare, the thematic groupings of private sector managers and their answers to the curiosity statements found by Kashdan et al. (2019) are Joyous Exploration (statements 1–4), Deprivation Sensitivity (statements 5–8), Stress Tolerance (statements 9–12), and Openness to People's Ideas (statements 13–16). In my analysis of public sector workers, the municipal public administrators, I found a single dominant grouping, including all of the statements, and a smaller grouping of opinions around lacking openness to people's ideas. Thus, it appears that the opinions of public sector workers fall along the following dimensions of opinion. Group 1 would be the curious administrators, strongly agreeing on curiosity across the index statements. The finding for Group 2 is an interesting contrarian result. Group 2 appears not to support the curiosity statements involving listening to others, valuing their opinions, and hearing the ideas of others. This small group represents an important non-curious theme among public administrators. There are two other groups from the factor analysis, but the opinions held in these groups are not as clearly expressed. Group 3 has significant loadings on two statements demonstrating that they let anxiety and distress affect their desire to be curious. Lastly, Group 4 seeks out tasks that include deep thought and getting excited thinking of new ideas, but there are no other strong sentiments of curiosity among the group.

Group 1: Curious Public Administrators
Group 2: Go-It-Alone Public Administrators
Group 3: Anxious Public Administrators
Group 4: Thoughtful Public Administrators

Group 1 fits within the theory of public administrative curiosity exposed in this book. It is the largest group among the respondents and the clearest loading, as shown by the large Eigenvalue of 5.4. The loadings for the other groups need to be interpreted with caution. Group 2, though, is interested in that they appear to be administrators against many sentiments of curiosity, especially the need to work with others. Group 3 appears to be administrators who are anxious when making decisions. Lastly, Group 4 only expressed curious sentiments in the area of thoughtfulness and not the others. While it is good that they are being thoughtful about decisions and enjoy exploring new ideas, the group needs to be more curious in not holding the same level of agreement with the other statements of curiosity. From the data analysis, there appear to be two clear groupings or themes, Curious Public Administrators and Go-It-Alone Public Administrators.

Public administrators appear to be more curious than private sector managers based on previous studies by Kashdan et al. (2019). The answers of the respondents in this chapter's survey loaded into two critical groups of opinion, with the strongest viewpoint being one of promoting curiosity in the workplace, whereas studies of the M-Workplace Curiosity Scale in private organizations show that private managers demonstrate more negative views of curiosity than their public sector counterparts (Kashdan et al., 2019).

To analyze curiosity as it pertains specifically to public administrators, I developed four statements based on the literature discussed in this book. The four statements were the last part of the survey administered to the study's sampled city managers. The statements are based on the need for compassion and empathy in curiosity, and that curiosity is about searching for evidence and answers and is vital. The statements are as follows.

1. *Public administrators need to practice compassion in their work.*
2. *Public administrators need to empathize with all members of their community.*
3. *The search for evidence in making decisions is one of the most essential parts of my job as a public administrator.*
4. *Being curious is vital to my success as a manager.*

Respondents were asked to rate their opinion of each statement on a scale of strongly agree (1) to strongly disagree (5). As shown in Table 4.5, the surveyed

Table 4.5 City Managers' Views on Curiosity

#	Statements	Minimum	Maximum	Mean	Std. Deviation	Variance	Count
1	Public administrators need to practice compassion in their work.	1.00	5.00	1.97	1.25	1.56	156
2	Public administrators need to empathize with all members of their community.	1.00	5.00	2.08	1.19	1.41	155
3	The search for evidence in making decisions is one of the most important parts of my job as a public administrator.	1.00	5.00	2.13	1.08	1.17	155
4	Being curious is vital to my success as a manager.	1.00	5.00	1.91	1.14	1.31	155

Source: Created by the author

Note: Please let us know your degree of agreement or disagreement with the following statements. Again, there is no right or wrong answer—ranging from strongly agree (1) to strongly disagree (5).

Table 4.6 City Managers' Views on Curiosity: Factor Analysis

	Component
	1
Public administrators need to practice compassion in their work.	.906
Public administrators need to empathize with all members of their community.	.892
The search for evidence in making decisions is one of the most important parts of my job as a public administrator.	.868
Being curious is vital to my success as a manager.	.886

Source: Created by the author

Note: Please let us know your degree of agreement or disagreement with the following statements. Again, there is no right or wrong answer—ranging from strongly agree (1) to strongly disagree (5). Significant loadings of 0.50 or higher are highlighted in yellow.

city managers supported curiosity as vital in public administration. The public administrators supported most of the ideas that curiosity is linked to compassion and that public administrators need to be compassionate along with the vitalness of curiosity to their work.

To understand the differences of opinion on the statements about curiosity and public administration, I conducted a component factor analysis of how the surveyed public administrators answered the four statements. Interestingly, as displayed in Table 4.6, the analysis only produced one grouping of opinions with an Eigenvalue of 3.155 and high loading values on the statements (.868 to .906), demonstrating a strongly held viewpoint that public administration and curiosity are linked. The data in Tables 4.5 and 4.6 support the assumptions in the public administration theory of curiosity that public administrators are compassionate, empathetic, evidence-orientated, and supportive of the idea that curiosity is a vital part of their work.

Predictors of Workplace Curiosity in the Public Sector

To determine the predictors and differences among the surveyed city managers, I conducted ordinary least squares (OLS) regression with an index of the M-Workplace Scale as the dependent variable. The variable was constructed by adding the answers of the respondents on the 16 statements for a total, with higher values being that the respondents expressed more curiosity. The independent variables of the OLS models were the type of position held by the respondent (i.e., city manager, city administrator), the form of government where the respondent worked, the region where the respondent's city is located, the population of the city, the age of the respondent, the gender of the respondent, and the type of degree held by the respondent. The OLS regression analysis found that the overall model of predictors was not strong and not statistically significant. The only independent variable with a statistically significant effect on workplace curiosity was the size of the city where the manager worked, with larger cities having managers with less curiosity.

Based on the factor analysis of the curiosity in workplace answers earlier in this chapter, I constructed a scale of the last four statements. I used it as a dependent variable to see if there were significant differences between respondents who were supported by curiosity involving interacting with others and respondents who were less supportive of this interpersonal feature of curiosity. The independent variables for this OLS model were the same as the ones used in the model discussed in the previous paragraph. The OLS regression of this scale as the dependent variable did not produce any significant results.

To summarize, I constructed two OLS models with the dependent variables being a scale of the two primary factor analysis groupings: those strongly supporting curiosity and those being cautious of interacting with others. Using a host of control questions and independent variables to identify meaningful differences among the respondents, I found that the population size of the city was the only variable to significant effect, and this was only in the first model explaining opinions on why managers were likely to be in the grouping of purely curious public administrators. And the finding is interesting in that it showed that larger cities had city managers who expressed less curiosity than the respondents working in smaller cities. Honestly, further study will be needed to explain this finding. Based on the literature reviewed in this book and the data presented, I hypothesize that city managers in smaller cities are limited in resources and recognize the need to be as curious as possible in their work to solve their administrative problems.

Conclusions on the Theory of the Curious Public Administrator

From the results of this chapter, though, we can make some general conclusions about how the book's theory of the curious public administrator applies to city managers.

First, overall, the city managers surveyed were strong supporters of the importance of curiosity in their work. Large majorities express support for curiosity, and most respondents are sorted as *Curious Public Administrators*.

Second, as noted, public administrators appear to be more curious than private sector managers. The answers of the respondents in this survey loaded into two key groups of opinion, with the strongest viewpoint being one of promoting curiosity in the workplace, whereas studies of the M-Workplace Curiosity Scale in private organizations show that private managers demonstrate more negative views of curiosity than their public sector counterparts.

Third, regression modeling showed no statistical relationships affecting how the surveyed public managers approach curiosity in the workplace. Gender, race, education, size of their cities, and other factors did not predict if managers were more curious in the public workplace. However, an interesting finding came from the analysis that public administrators leading smaller cities were likelier to express stronger support for curiosity in their work.

Future research on curiosity in public administration needs to focus on administering more curiosity in workplace instruments to public administrators at the state or federal levels. These studies need to collect more qualitative data on curiosity in the public workplace. And next, we will examine how public administrator faculty approach curiosity in their teaching and research.

References

Alexander, S. (2015). *Female city managers in Texas: A content analysis of resumes to identify successful career path trends.* Applied Research Project, Texas State University. Retrieved from https://digital.library.txstate.edu/bitstream/handle/10877/5 886/ AlexanderS amantha.pdf?sequence=1&isAllowed=y

Alkadry, M. G., Bishu, S. G., & Ali, S. B. (2019). Beyond representation: Gender, authority, and city managers. *Review of Public Personnel Administration, 39*(2), 300–319.

Ammons, D. N., & Bosse, M. J. (2005). Tenure of city managers: Examining the dual meanings of "average tenure". *State and Local Government Review, 37*(1), 61–71.

Beaty, L., & Davis, T. J. (2012). Gender disparity in professional city management: Making the case for enhancing leadership curriculum. *Journal of Public Affairs Education, 18*(4), 617–632.

Dolamore, S. (2021). Detecting empathy in public organizations: Creating a more relational public administration. *Administrative Theory & Praxis, 43*(1), 58–81.

Feeney, M. K., & Camarena, L. (2021). Gender, race, and diversity values among local government leaders. *Review of Public Personnel Administration, 41*(1), 105–131.

Folz, D. H., & French, P. E. (2005). *Managing America's small communities: People, politics, and performance.* Rowman & Littlefield.

Fox, R. L., & Schuhmann, R. A. (1999). Gender and local government: A comparison of women and men city managers. *Public Administration Review, 59*(3), 231–242.

Frederickson, H. G., Johnson, G. A., & Wood, C. (2004). The changing structure of American cities: A study of the diffusion of innovation. *Public Administration Review, 64*(3), 320–330.

Hatcher, W., Rauhaus, B., & Meares, W. L. (2022). The career paths of the chief administrative officers of US cities: A survey of city managers and content analysis of how they discuss their careers. *Local Government Studies,* 1–21.

Holman, M. (2017). Women in Local Government: What we know and where we go from here. *State and Local Government Review, 49*(4), 285–296.

International City/County Management Association (ICMA). (2015). *Municipal Year Book.* Washington, D.C.: ICMA.

Kashdan, T. B., Goodman, F. R., Disabato, D. J., McKnight, P. E., Kelso, K., & Naughton, C. (2020). Curiosity has comprehensive benefits in the workplace: Developing and validating a multidimensional workplace curiosity scale in United States and German employees. *Personality and Individual Differences, 155,* 109717.

Kellogg, L. D., Gourrier, A. G., Bernick, E. L., & Brekken, K. (2019). County governing boards: Where are all the women? *Politics, Groups, and Identities, 7*(1), 39–51.

Kruyen, P. M., & van Genugten, M. (2017). Creativity in local government: Definition and determinants. *Public Administration, 95*(3), 825–841.

Moynihan, D. P., & Landuyt, N. (2009). How do public organizations learn? Bridging cultural and structural perspectives. *Public Administration Review, 69*(6), 1097–1105.

National League of Cities. (N/D). Forms of Municipal Government. Retrieved from https://www.nlc.org/forms-of-municipal-government.

Perry, J. L. (1997). Antecedents of public service motivation. *Journal of Public Administration Research and Theory, 7*(2), 181–197.

Ritz, A., Brewer, G. A., & Neumann, O. (2016). Public service motivation: A systematic literature review and outlook. *Public Administration Review, 76*(3), 414–426.

Stone, D. C. (1981). Innovative organizations require innovative managers. *Public Administration Review, 41*(5), 507–513.

Watson, D. J., & Hassett, W. L. (2003). Long–serving city managers: Why do they stay? *Public Administration Review, 63*(1), 71–78.

Watson, D. J., & Hassett, W. L. (2004). Career Paths of city managers in America's Largest council-manager cities. *Public Administration Review, 64*(2), 192–199.

5 Curious Public Administration Faculty

This chapter focuses on how faculty view curiosity and how they teach the concept to current and future public administrators. Why do I dedicate an entire chapter to the views of public administration faculty? Public administration is a professional and scholarly field that needs to connect theory with practice, and this linkage often occurs in the classroom. Thus, faculty need to be effective instructors to advance empirical findings from scholarly journals and books to the classrooms and, hopefully, to improve public administration in practice. However, scholarship on teaching and learning is often less respected than research in other areas of public administration. This is an issue for the field if we need to ensure that faculty in our classrooms are properly trained based on the latest research to do their best to connect theory with practice for their students. Fortunately, McDonald (2023) demonstrated that research on teaching and learning is read and cited more than research in other subfields of public administration. The results discussed in this chapter contribute to the field's scholarship of teaching and learning and, in doing so, extend the theory of the curious public administrator to the classroom.

This chapter collects primary data from researchers and instructors who teach in NASPAA member programs of public affairs. The survey instrument asks faculty to provide their viewpoints regarding researching the concept of curiosity and how to teach curiosity in public affairs programs. To recap, curiosity is defined as *the intellectual motivation to objectively learn how the world works* (Hatcher, 2019a, 2019b; Inan, 2013). Like the instrument administered to city managers, the survey approaches curiosity based on this definition and the theory of the curious public administrator detailed in Chapter 3. Furthermore, as noted, the survey to faculty in public administration includes the M-Workplace Curiosity questions.

This chapter's survey was emailed to nearly 2,700 faculty who teach in the Network of Schools of Public Policy, Affairs, and Administration (NASPAA), member schools, and public affairs programs. As noted, the survey asks the public affairs faculty their viewpoint on curiosity, their opinions about the importance of curiosity to public administration, and their ideas about instruction methods to illustrate the concept. The survey also collects data through

DOI: 10.4324/9781032668826-5

control questions asking the faculty their academic rank, tenure status, educational background, career experience as practitioners, and demographics. Additionally, the instrument included questions about the programs where the faculty teach, such as the number of students, the program's concentrations, and whether the program is housed in a research institution or not. The survey data are analyzed by descriptive statistics, content analysis of open-ended questions, crosstabs, factor analysis, and regression.

Surveying Public Administration Faculty

To examine how public administration faculty research and teach curiosity, I constructed a survey instrument to collect data from faculty in NASPAA member programs. The survey contains 49 questions that collect data in the following areas: the characteristics of the faculty and their programs, the demographics of the faculty, their definitions of curiosity as a concept, and their viewpoints of curiosity in the workplace and the field of public administration. The survey includes the same 16-question instrument administered to city managers in Chapter 4. In Chapter 4, this instrument is used in assessing the curiosity levels of the local public managers in the study. As noted in Chapter 3, the instrument is a standardized and validated survey from the research literature on curiosity. Kashdan et al. (2020) developed the instrument to assess the multiple dimensions of curiosity in the workplace. The authors titled the instrument the M-Workplace Curiosity Scale. This chapter's survey expands the literature by administering the M-Workplace Curiosity Scale to public administration faculty members.

I administered the survey to faculty members working in academic programs, departments, and/or schools affiliated as members of the NASPAA, the global accrediting body for public administration. The survey was administered by using an email database of NASPAA faculty. The database contained 2,645 faculty who received the survey. The survey was administered via Qualtrics through emails in multiple waves between June 28, 2022 and

Table 5.1 Characteristics and Demographics of the Study's Sample of NASPAA Faculty Members

Category	Variable	N	Valid %
Position Type ($N = 281$)	Lecturer/Instructor	22	7.83
	Assistant Professor	33	11.74
	Associate Professor	83	29.54
	Professor	123	43.77
	Other	20	7.12
Region ($N = 278$)	Northeast	65	23.38
	South	103	37.05
	Midwest	58	20.86
	West	52	18.71

(Continued)

Table 5.1 (Continued)

Category	Variable	N	Valid %
Tenure Status (*N* = 281)	Tenured	199	70.82
	Not tenured but tenure track	24	8.54
	Not tenured and not tenure track	58	20.64
Administrative Position	Yes	122	43.57
(*N* = 280)	No	158	56.43
Gender (*N* = 281)	Female	112	39.86
	Male	168	59.79
	Prefer not to say	1	0.36
Age (*N* = 281)	25–34	3	1.74
	35–44	54	19.22
	45–54	77	27.40
	55–64	69	24.56
	65 and older	76	27.05
	Prefer not to say	2	0.71
Race (*N* = 170)	American Indian or Alaska Native	3	1.10
	Asian	18	6.62
	Black or African American	16	5.88
	White	235	86.40
University Status (*N* = 173)	Teaching-orientated institution	46	16.55
	Moving toward a research-orientated institution	72	25.90
	Clearly a research-orientated institution	160	57.55
Teaching Load of MPA	2/2	145	51.79
Faculty (*N* = 173)	3/3	80	28.57
	4/4	16	5.71
	5/5	1	0.36
	Other	38	13.57

Source: Created by the author

Note: Based on the U.S. Census, the states in each region are as follows: **Northeast** = Connecticut, Maine, Massachusetts, New Hampshire, New Jersey, New York, Pennsylvania, Rhode Island, and Vermont; **South** = Alabama, Arkansas, Delaware, District of Columbia, Florida, Georgia, Kentucky, Louisiana, Maryland, Mississippi, North Carolina, Oklahoma, South Carolina, Tennessee, Texas, Virginia, and West Virginia; **Midwest** = Illinois, Indiana, Iowa, Kansas, Michigan, Minnesota, Missouri, Nebraska, North Dakota, Ohio, South Dakota, and Wisconsin; **West** = Alaska, Arizona, California, Colorado, Hawaii, Idaho, Montana, Nevada, New Mexico, Oregon, Washington, and Wyoming.

July 28, 2022. Of the 2,645 faculty contacted by email, 329 started the survey, with most of this group completing it, which is a response rate of 12.4%.

The Study's Surveyed Faculty

The 329 surveyed faculty comprise a representative sample of NASPAA faculty. The characteristics of the faculty and their institutions provide insightful data on the state of the field's academic programs. The first interesting finding is that, of the surveyed faculty, most were senior faculty with tenure. For instance, a plurality of surveyed faculty (43.77%) were identified as Full Professors. Seventy percent of the surveyed faculty indicated that they tenured. It appears that the survey oversampled tenured faculty. However, this chapter's survey included a similar percentage of tenured professors as other published surveys of NASPAA faculty. Knepper et al. (2020) found that 71.2% of the surveyed NASPAA faculty in their study were tenured. Faculty were asked to identify the region of their home institutions. The largest percentage of surveyed faculty (37.05%) were identified as working in universities in the South.

Of the surveyed faculty in this chapter's study, a large percentage (43.57%) reported having administration experience, which is unsurprising given the nature of the field and how faculty are often asked to serve as a program, department, or school leader. Close to 60% of the surveyed faculty identified as men, slightly higher than the percentage of faculty identifying as men selected for samples of similar surveys (Knepper et al., 2020). The imbalance in favor of men is worrisome, given that most students in and graduates of MPA programs are identified as women (Beaty & Davis, 2012).

Another worrisome trend for a field that needs to promote diversity in public institutions is the need for racial diversity among the surveyed faculty. Eighty-six percent of people were identified as white. Unfortunately, this result is similar to surveys of academic programs conducted by NASPAA. For example, during the 2019–2020 academic year, 77% of NASPAA faculty were identified as white (NASPAA, 2020). While not the focus of this chapter and the overall book, it is important to note that the field needs to practice what it preaches in advancing diversity among its faculty. With a large number of the field's faculty entering the end stages of their career, there is an opportunity for academic programs, departments, and schools to diversify their faculty ranks to ensure that the public administration academy is reflective of the students that they teach and the public institutions that they serve. For example, in 2019–2020, 40% of the students enrolled in NASPAA programs were identified as minorities, compared to 23% of the faculty that year (NASPAA, 2020).

Lastly, I wanted to identify the types of institutions (teaching or research) where faculty worked to see if the characteristics of their home institutions affect their viewpoints on curiosity in public administration. There are over 300 NASPAA member programs in academic institutions ranging from teaching-focused universities, where faculty regularly teach four courses per semester, to research-orientated universities, where faculty may teach two or fewer courses per semester. Most of the surveyed faculty (57.55%) identified working at a research-oriented institution, with a smaller majority (51.79%) indicating that they typically teach two courses per semester. The survey sample may include an oversampling of faculty working at research-orientated institutions. However, on the other hand, this is a notable finding which may demonstrate that faculty are receiving needed support for research. Even NASPAA faculty working in small MPA programs (100 or fewer students) indicate having support for research (Hatcher et al., 2017).

NASPAA Faculty and Curiosity

Regarding curiosity in the workplace and the answers of the faculty respondents on the M-Workplace Curiosity instrument, NASPAA faculty highly support curiosity in their work. Table 5.2 shows the mean scores on each statement. Faculty agreed the most with the statements regarding valuing the opinions of others. Table 5.3 presents the factor analysis results of how respondents answered the M-Workplace Curiosity statements. The groupings of opinion among NASPAA faculty are similar to the city managers surveyed in Chapter 4. There is one strong grouping of curiosity, but the other two

Table 5.2 Curiosity in the Academic Workplace: Faculty

#	Field	Minimum	Maximum	Mean	Std. Deviation	Variance	Count
1	I enjoy that I often find my mind continues to work through complex problems outside of work.	1.00	5.00	3.91	0.95	0.90	265
2	I get excited thinking about experimenting with different ideas.	1.00	5.00	4.00	0.99	0.98	265
3	At work, I seek out opportunities to expand my knowledge or skills.	1.00	5.00	3.88	1.01	1.02	265
4	I seek out work tasks where I will have to think in-depth about something.	1.00	5.00	3.79	0.99	0.98	265
5	When given a complex problem at work, I can't rest until I find the answer.	1.00	5.00	3.42	1.09	1.19	265
6	When a complex work problem arises, I continue to seek information until I understand it fully.	1.00	5.00	3.85	0.96	0.91	264
7	I can spend hours on a single problem because I feel a need to find an answer.	1.00	5.00	3.50	1.12	1.25	265

8 I work relentlessly to find answers to complicated questions at work.	1.00	5.00	3.37	1.08	1.16	265
9 When work is anxiety provoking, I tend to explore rather than avoid.	1.00	5.00	3.08	1.04	1.09	263
10 The possibility of being distressed does not impact my motivation to work on new projects.	1.00	5.00	3.15	1.19	1.42	264
11 I do not shy away from the unknown or unfamiliar even if it seems scary.	1.00	5.00	3.66	1.09	1.19	265
12 When probing deeper into a project that interests me, feeling anxious does not derail me.	1.00	5.00	3.52	1.13	1.29	264
13 It is important to listen to ideas from people who think differently.	1.00	5.00	4.32	1.00	1.00	265
14 I value colleagues with different ideas.	1.00	5.00	4.22	0.99	0.99	265
15 I like to hear ideas from colleagues even if they are different from my current line of thinking.	1.00	5.00	4.17	1.00	0.99	265
16 Even when I am confident in my approach to a problem, I like to hear other people's opinions.	1.00	5.00	4.14	0.99	0.99	265

Source: Created by the author

Note: Here are statements people often use to describe themselves. Thinking of your job and your workplace, please indicate the degree to which each statement has been characteristic of you. There are no right or wrong answers—ranging from very slightly or not at all (1) to extremely (5).

Table 5.3 Curiosity in the Academic Workplace: Factor Analysis

	Component		
	1	*2*	*3*
I get excited thinking about experimenting with different ideas.	.781	−.004	.069
At work, I seek out opportunities to expand my knowledge or skills.	.769	.086	.072
I seek out work tasks where I will have to think in-depth about something.	.767	.069	.059
When given a complex problem at work, I can't rest until I find the answer.	.668	.379	−.407
When a complex work problem arises, I continue to seek information until I understand it fully.	.806	.114	−.288
I can spend hours on a single problem because I feel a need to find an answer.	.593	.181	−.567
I work relentlessly to find answers to complicated questions at work.	.690	.340	−.446
When work is anxiety provoking, I tend to explore rather than avoid.	.550	.460	.070
The possibility of being distressed does not impact my motivation to work on new projects.	.503	.471	.491
I do not shy away from the unknown or unfamiliar even if it seems scary.	.663	.071	.527
When probing deeper into a project that interests me, feeling anxious does not derail me.	.513	.284	.587
It is important to listen to ideas from people who think differently.	.793	−.486	.052
I value colleagues with different ideas.	.801	−.497	.044
I like to hear ideas from colleagues even if they are different from my current line of thinking.	.823	−.439	−.028
Even when I am confident in my approach to a problem, I like to hear other people's opinions.	.785	−.433	.005

Source: Created by the author

Note: Here are statements people often use to describe themselves. Thinking of your job and your workplace, please indicate the degree to which each statement has been characteristic of you. There are no right or wrong answers—ranging from very slightly or not at all (1) to extremely (5).
Extraction Method: Principal Component Analysis.[a]
[a] Three components extracted.

groupings or themes are not coherent based on a review of their loadings on each statement.

Tables 5.4 and 5.5 report the faculty's viewpoints on curiosity in their academic work, the classroom, and the field's curricula. Regarding how curiosity is taught in the public administration curricula, the NASPAA faculty can be put into two groups. One that supports and thinks curiosity can be taught in MPA classes and another smaller group that does not think that curiosity can be easily taught.

Table 5.4 Faculty Views on Curiosity

#	Field	Minimum	Maximum	Mean	Std. Deviation	Variance	Count
1	Public administrators need to practice compassion in their work.	1.00	5.00	1.68	1.00	1.00	250
2	Public administrators need to empathize with all members of their community.	1.00	5.00	1.78	1.02	1.05	251
3	The search for evidence in making decisions is one of the most important being a public administrator.	1.00	5.00	1.89	1.01	1.02	250
4	Being curious is vital to being successful as a public administrator.	1.00	5.00	2.02	1.01	1.02	250
5	Curiosity should be included in the curriculum of public affairs programs.	1.00	5.00	2.51	1.08	1.16	249
6	Curiosity is a concept that cannot be easily taught in the classroom.	1.00	5.00	2.46	1.16	1.35	250
7	Practicing curiosity in their jobs causes public administrators to be politically biased in their work.	1.00	5.00	3.91	1.14	1.31	249

Source: Created by the author

Note: Please let us know your degree of agreement or disagreement with the following statements. Again, there is no right or wrong answer—ranging from strongly agree (1) to strongly disagree (5).

Table 5.5 Faculty' Views on Curiosity: Factor Analysis

	Component	
	1	2
Public administrators need to practice compassion in their work.	.875	−.016
Public administrators need to empathize with all members of their community.	.853	−.072
The search for evidence in making decisions is one of the most important being a public administrator.	.758	.051
Being curious is vital to being successful as a public administrator.	.842	−.028

(Continued)

Table 5.5 (Continued)

	Component	
	1	*2*
Curiosity should be included in the curriculum of public affairs programs.	.691	.107
Curiosity is a concept that cannot be easily taught in the classroom.	.225	.741
Practicing curiosity in their jobs causes public administrators to be politically biased in their work.	−.240	.749

Source: Created by the author

Note: Please let us know your degree of agreement or disagreement with the following statements. Again, there is no right or wrong answer—ranging from strongly agree (1) to strongly disagree (5).
Extraction Method: Principal Component Analysis.[a]
[a]   Two components extracted.

Predictors of Workplace Curiosity Among Faculty

As in the previous chapter, I constructed a scale for the M-Workplace Curiosity statements and used it as a dependent variable in an OLS regression analysis. The independent variables for the OLS regression model to explain predictors of workplace curiosity among faculty were: faculty rank, tenure status, whether they hold an administrative position, the region where their institution is located, gender, age, and whether they work at a teaching-focused or research-orientated institution. The OLS regression analysis found little evidence. Overall, the model was statistically significant, but the R-squared value was small, showing little explanation power of variance in workplace curiosity. Interestingly, the only significant variable in the model was whether the faculty held an administrative position. The faculty who held an administrative position demonstrated more curiosity in their opinions of the M-Workplace Curiosity statements than faculty who did not hold an administrative post. Faculty who take the leap to administrative positions may be more open to change, which is a critical component of curiosity.

The following sections attempt to unpack and explain these findings by examining open-ended comments left by NASPAA faculty.

Defining and Teaching Curiosity

I asked three open-ended questions to provide a rich description of how NASPAA faculty view curiosity and how they incorporate the concept into their courses and MPA programs.

1. How would you define curiosity?
2. Can you describe an assignment in your classes that teaches students how to practice curiosity in the public workplace?
3. Please identify the classes in a typical MPA program that you think are the most important courses for teaching curiosity in public administration.

In this section, I analyze their answers, present themes in the data, and end with a discussion of assignments and classes that help students learn and practice curiosity.

1. Defining Curiosity

To understand how faculty approach curiosity in their classrooms and with their scholarly work, I compare their definitions of the concept with the one I developed based on the literature. Again, to recap that definition, curiosity is defined as *the intellectual motivation to objectively learn how the world works* (Hatcher, 2019a, 2019b; Inan, 2013). When asked how they define the concept, the surveyed faculty discussed curiosity as asking "why," seeking to solve puzzles, desiring to understand how the world works, and other ways of building knowledge and learning. I used NVivo to identify the top word frequencies and how the respondents were discussing those concepts. The top five words were *desire, know, interest, something,* and *learn*.

To learn more about how faculty define curiosity, I conducted a word tree analysis of the top words used by faculty. Looking at the word tree of how faculty used the word "desire" to define curiosity demonstrates a focus on viewing curiosity as having an unsatiable drive to know, understand, learn, seek, and explore how the world works. The word trees of the other top words show similar results, leading me to assert that faculty define curiosity similar to the literature and the definition used in this book.

2. Teaching Curiosity

The questions on teaching curiosity focus on how faculty approach the concept in their classrooms and their views on how the concept is taught (and should be taught) across the public administration curriculum. When asked how they approach curiosity in their classrooms, many faculty members discussed assignments. The top words used by faculty when discussing assignments were students, public, problem, research, and questions. Content analyses of these statements and word trees show that the assignments involve identifying problems and finding solutions, case studies, building theories, and critical thinking analyses. Here, I include examples of the assignments and how the faculty discussed them.

Case studies are good for curiosity. One case study was on parking fees, whether they should be changed and how the different parking lots should be structured to negatively impact the least number of residents. Curious students actually looked at other parking fees and lots in other cities in order to answer the questions in the case and to develop their fees. Other students just answered the questions and used no other sources, just what was in their brain at the time that they did the assignments.

I have a neighborhood inventory that cause students to explore their neighborhoods.

I look for ways to push students to engage in critical thinking—which I view as akin to engaging curiosity. Critical thinking encourages students to "think outside the box" and apply the information they are receiving in new, different, and sometimes unfamiliar ways. The curious student is oftentimes the one who best excels in engaging in critical thinking.

One of the most useful ways to inculcate curiosity, is to note how much of public administration is counter-intuitive. For example, the concept of politics is multi-dimensional. Public administration conceptually is a political practice with those in and above middle management being political actors as well as managers and administrators. And they should be professional politicians, that is, profess critical political values around our city charters, constitutions and laws. By confronting the conceptual complexity of public administration, curiosity is inevitably piqued as students when wonder why such distinctions are often not noted or handled well.

Developing a problem statement of observed problems in their workplace including the history of how it came to be. Then write a theory based change plan to address the problem, including projecting probable consequences.

A common theme throughout the data was how faculty noted the need for little guidance in their assignments for students to find their way through coursework to curiosity. For example, a faculty member stated, "Give them a problem that has multiple factors and solutions to see was sort of creative or curious inquiry might emerge." Another faculty wrote, "I give them ambiguous assignments and push them to pursue answers to these questions. Trying to prepare them for tackling these questions that have no clear answer." This practice for teaching abstract concepts for public administration is supported in the field's literature on teaching and learning. For instance, Merritt et al. (2018) utilized assignments with minimum guidance to teach the publicness theory successfully.

Another common theme throughout the discussion is the emphasis on case studies as a tool for teaching curiosity in the public administration classroom. There are examples in the literature on teaching and learning of how faculty use case studies to teach abstract concepts from leadership (Beckett, 1997) to ethics (Cram & Alkadry, 2018). A faculty member described using case studies to teach curiosity by focusing on the connection with thinking and writing. As the faculty member wrote, "Discussing case studies and writing memos encourages creativity, which could lead to or foster curiosity." Another faculty member simply stated, "I often use case studies which often requires creative thinking." Another wrote, "any good case study" will help promote curiosity. Faculty noted that using case studies encouraged considering multiple solutions from numerous frameworks. As a faculty described it, "I use case studies with a multiple perspectives framework that I think is well suited to complex public sector problems." Overall, it appears the faculty think that case studies help teach curiosity because the assignments require students to consider how the world works in a manner where there are several or many correct approaches to analyze complex problems and in the several or many appropriate answers. The top words used by faculty when discussing public administration curricula and classes were policy, research, methods, management, and ethics. Analysis of the word trees associated with these top words shows that curiosity is taught in the foundation/introduction to public administration classes, public policy, research methods, and capstone courses. The faculty discussed using public policy class the most to demonstrate curiosity in making decisions. Research methods and the introduction to public administration and management courses were also some of the top ones pointed to as courses for the locus of curiosity in the curricula of MPA programs. Conversely, faculty mentioned that budgeting focusing on rules of accounting, revenue, auditing, and financing might not be the most appropriate topic for teaching curiosity. On the other hand, several faculty strongly stressed that every class in the MPA curriculum could be used to teach curiosity. I include here some of the discussions from the faculty on how they see curiosity integrated across the MPA curriculum.

> Introduction to PA [public administration], looking at how modern PA is a product of the reform movement yet informed by practitioners such as Alexander Hamilton. Strategic administration is another critical course for curiosity as complex organizations, a characteristic of most public agencies, are counter-intuitive. This demands multi-dimensional administration to create and protect efficient task performance, nurture future constitutional administrators and forge the politics into a productive and mutual interaction with the specific publics, such as the media, and the general public.
>
> Public Administration Ethics and Organization Theory (because students are prone to think in very conventional terms about core issues in both courses).
>
> Intro to pa [public administration], methods classes (including statistics—how to answer questions), all of them—one PA failure is the failure to anticipate unintended consequences (e.g. of policy decisions)— students need to be encouraged to understand how their decisions will affect those impacted, which implies/requires curiosity.
>
> Every course can have a focus on being curious about the unknown, and discussing the anxiety of asking for help, and creating a sufficiently trusting work environment where it is safe to say, "I don't know."

Interestingly, a small number of faculty strongly argued that curiosity could not be taught in the public administration classroom. They compared curiosity to a "personal trait" and not a skill. As one faculty member wrote:

It's not clear to me that this [curiosity] should be a teaching goal unless curiosity is being used to mean thoroughness in investigating options and alternatives. That is, curiosity is a great personal trait but it may not be a skill.

It should be stressed that this opinion is not widely shared throughout the statements made by public administration faculty, but it is an important critique of teaching curiosity. The viewpoint is that certain aspects of administration are personal traits and thus cannot be taught in the classroom.

This is an argument that was widely used against teaching leadership in public administration programs (Denhardt & Campbell, 2018). But for decades, it has been commonly accepted that leadership can be taught in our classes, with many programs even having individual courses dedicated solely to leadership. This has occurred because the idea that there are personal traits of being a leader has been disproven (Denhardt & Campbell, 2005). This arguably can also be said for the view that curiosity is a trait rather than a concept that can be taught. The vast majority of faculty surveyed agreed with the statement that curiosity is a topic of concern for public administration courses.

Assessing the Teaching of Curiosity

Now that I have covered how faculty approach curiosity in their work, how they define the concept, and how they teach the concept in our public administration classroom, I want to leave the reader with a step-by-step guide I developed to teach curiosity across the public administration curriculum. I have written in *Teaching Public Administration* (2019b) about incorporating curiosity in public administration courses and across MPA programs. The teaching of curiosity can be aligned with NASPAA's five competencies. I have included a few examples here.

NASPAA Competency 1: Lead and manage in public governance.

Exercise: Students interview a local public manager and reflect on how they practice empathy and curiosity in their work.
Teaches: Empathy's role in curiosity.

NASPAA Competency 2: Participate in and contribute to the policy process.

Exercise: Students select a policy and write a reflective paper on how the policy affects community residents.
Teaches: Empathy's role in curiosity.

NASPAA Competency 3: Analyze, synthesize, think critically, solve problems, and make decisions.

Exercise: Students analyze performance measurements developed by a governmental agency and reflect on if the measures achieve outcomes.

Teaches: The desire to solve problems effectively.

NASPAA Competency 4: Articulate and apply a public service perspective.

Exercise: Students will develop a public engagement plan for a city's comprehensive planning process.

Teaches: The need to integrate the public in decision-making to develop effective solutions. Empathy's role in curiosity.

NASPAA Competency 5: Communicate and interact productively with a diverse and changing workforce and citizenry.

Exercise: Students analyze the demographic composition of a local government and reflect on if it is representative of the community being served.

Teaches: The need for public bureaucracies to be representative of the communities that they serve. Empathy's role in curiosity.

These example exercises can be taught across the typical curriculum of MPA programs. For instance, having students apply empathy to the decisions of public managers can be the foundation of assignments in an introduction to public administration course, a leadership course, an evaluation course, a policy formulation and implementation course, and many others in the MPA curriculum. The commonalities across curiosity-based exercises are a focus on illustrating empathy, a need to involve the public to learn how the world works, an emphasis on finding answers, and a concern for reflection in an objective manner.

Concluding Thoughts

This chapter presented crucial data for achieving the goals of this book, particularly developing an administrative theory of curiosity for the public sector. Knowing the viewpoints of public administration faculty regarding curiosity in scholarship and teaching comprises these crucial data. Through analyzing these data, we found that public administration faculty are highly curious in the workplace. The faculty define curiosity in terms of talking about wanting to know how public administration works. The public administration faculty mostly held the viewpoint that curiosity could be taught in the public administration classroom, particularly in courses focusing on leadership and policy analysis. Lastly, using the data analyzed in this chapter and previous work (Hatcher, 2019b), I sketch some examples of how faculty can teach curiosity in public administration courses.

References

Beaty, L., & Davis, T. J. (2012). Gender disparity in professional city management: Making the case for enhancing leadership curriculum. *Journal of Public Affairs Education, 18*(4), 617–632.

Beckett, J. (1997). Skirting the swamp: Using case studies for developing leadership skills. *Journal of Public Administration Education, 3*(2), 235–238.

Cram, B., & Alkadry, M. (2018). Virtue ethics and cultural competence: Improving service one administrator at a time. *Journal of Public Affairs Education, 24*(4), 518–537.

Denhardt, J. V., & Campbell, K. B. (2005). Leadership education in public administration: Finding the fit between purpose and approach. *Journal of Public Affairs Education, 11*(3), 169–179.

Hatcher, W. (2019a). The curious public administrator: The new administrative doctrine. *Public Integrity, 21*(3), 225–228.

Hatcher, W. (2019b). Teaching curiosity in public affairs programs. *Teaching Public Administration, 37*(3), 365–375.

Hatcher, W., Meares, W. L., & Gordon, V. (2017). The capacity and constraints of small MPA programs: A survey of program directors. *Journal of Public Affairs Education, 23*(3), 855–868.

Inan, I. (2013). *The philosophy of curiosity.* Routledge.

Knepper, H. J., Scutelnicu, G., & Tekula, R. (2020). Why gender and research productivity matters in academia: Exploring evidence from NASPAA-accredited schools. *Journal of Public Affairs Education, 26*(1), 51–72.

McDonald III, B. D. (2023). The dark horse of public administration: The challenge of pedagogical research. *Teaching Public Administration, 41*(1).

Merritt, C. C., Farnworth, M. D., & Kienapple, M. R. (2018). Developing organizational leaders to manage publicness: A conceptual framework. *Journal of Public Affairs Education, 24*(2), 216–233.

NASPAA. (2020). *NASPAA annual data report.* Retrieved from www.naspaa.org/sites/default/files/docs/2021-09/ADR%202019-2020_KM_FINAL.pdf

6 Curiosity in Public Organizations

The book has covered the literature on curiosity, positioned the research in public administration, and developed a framework for curiosity in public administration. This framework guided the collection and analysis of primary data from public administrators and faculty who teach in public affairs programs. Next, this chapter details the features of successful public agencies to determine whether these public organizations are demonstrating features of curiosity at the institutional level. I examined federal agencies identified through the Office of Personnel Management's (OPM) annual survey and analyzed by the Partnership for Public Service as their "Best Places to Work" survey and ranking (Partnership for Public Service, 2020). After this discussion, I move on to public organizations at the state and local level that have demonstrated features of curiosity or have lacked an organizational approach to curiosity.

The OPM surveys federal employees on many measures that represent high performance in public agencies, including leadership effectiveness, work-life balance, pay, innovation, teamwork, and other indicators of successful units. In 2020, the survey identified the following top agencies:

1. National Aeronautics and Space Administration (NASA)
2. Intelligence Community
3. Department of Transportation
4. Department of Health and Human Services
5. Department of Commerce[1]

Using the lens of the administrative theory of curiosity, I examine three of these agencies—NASA, the Department of Transportation, and the Department of Health and Human Services. Given the nature of the Intelligence Community, which includes multiple agencies working in secrecy, I focus on the other three agencies. Next, I talk about some of the features of public organizations that may lack curiosity. After that discussion, this chapter moves to align the features of curious organizations with the public administration literature.

DOI: 10.4324/9781032668826-6

Features of Curiosity Among the Top Federal Workplaces

Highly Educated Workforces

When thinking about the workplaces in NASA, the Department of Transportation, and the Department of Health and Human Services, one commonality stands out, the professional nature of the employees. Many of the employees in these organizations are highly educated and what McGregor (1960) termed "Theory Y" employees, working in positions dealing with information and creativity. These workplaces are occupied by engineers, scientists, medical doctors, and others in professions typically focused on understanding how the world works, in other words, curiosity. The educated workforces of these agencies fit within the overall federal employment, with 25% of the federal workforce holding advanced degrees in 2017 (OPM, 2017).

While the federal workforce overall is highly educated, the agencies of NASA, Transportation, and Health and Human Services are even more educated than the general workforce. For instance, in NASA, approximately 80% of the agency's permanent staff members hold PhD (NASA, 2021); in the Department of Transportation, which probably has the lowest education levels of the three agencies, over 28% of the workforce holds at least a bachelor's degree; and in the Department of Health and Human Services, over 13,542 employees hold doctorates and 17,733 hold master's degrees (OPM, 2022).

Creativity

In these agencies, especially in NASA and Health and Human Services, there is learning how things work and applying that knowledge to make improvements in exploring space, building infrastructure, and providing public programs focused on the health and well-being of the nation's residents. Due to decades of rhetoric bashing the government, the public tends not to think of public administration as creative. But many within government at all levels are highly creative in their work and solutions to public problems. Moreover, the creativity of employees is an essential factor in determining organizational learning and performance in both private and public organizations (Eldor & Harpaz, 2019).

Still, the research on creativity in the public sector is limited. Houtgraff, Kruyen, and Thiel (2023) reviewed the literature, and based on their definition of creativity, "public servants coming up with novel and useful ideas through various practices," found a need for the field to study the topic in greater detail (p. 1). However, my review of the literature found research, albeit dated, that can help advance our understanding of creativity in the public sector. West and Berman (1997) found a strong focus on creativity in the public sector if the term is considered problem-solving. Similarly, Cates (1979) argued for creativity to help with decision-making processes and move public organizations away from the process of muddling through or incrementalism toward more strategic and rational decision-making.

Conversely, Rangarajan (2008) found that governmental units recognized with the Innovation of Government Awards were likely to make incremental improvements. The author applied two models of public sector creativity to come to this conclusion. First, the Sternberg (1999) model focuses on creativity in public sector outcomes, and second, the Unsworth (2001) model of creativity at the various levels of government.

Throughout the literature on creativity is a concern with problem-solving, which is the same as what we have discussed about curiosity in public administration, leading to the assumption that there can be a connection between the two concepts in successful public organizations.

Diversity

Compared to other parts of the federal workforce and state and local governments, these three agencies are diverse in gender and race. The importance of diversity and social equity is argued throughout the public administration literature, and thankfully for democracy and human rights, diversity and social equity have become key features of public administration theory and practice. However, public administration theory and practice often are too concerned with "getting things done" at the expense of equity (Alkadry et al., 2017). Curiosity, as described in this book, may help mediate this problem by encouraging decision-makers to be empathetic and try to put themselves in the shoes of the people affected by their policies and practices. To be truly curious, one has to be interested and care about those who are different from them, and perhaps agencies with diversity encourage this outcome more than homogenous agencies.

Mission-Orientated

Another feature in how these federal agencies stand out is their focus on mission. In his book *Mission Mystique*, Goodsell (2010) effectively argues that public agencies that achieve positive outcomes—like helping people experiencing homelessness, feeding people experiencing poverty, and protecting children—are organizations with employees seeking to put beliefs in place around their passions. These are agencies focused on mission, not just implemented laws. This view of agencies being vehicles for missions and the passions of their workers fits within the administrative curiosity theory of this book. And as can be seen, the agencies discussed in this chapter (NASA, USDOT, and USHHS) are often focused on missions around exploring space, building infrastructure, and protecting the health and security of Americans and not simply implementing laws.

Know How to Involve the Public

Curious individuals and, in turn, curious organizations naturally need to be interested in learning what others think about a given issue or problem. They want to collect information to answer questions about how the world works. This requires soliciting viewpoints and opinions from the public. Thus, it can be asserted that curious organizations want to involve the public in their decision-making processes. There is research supporting this claim. For instance, cities with workers with more of an accountability approach to government are more likely to support public participation in decision-making processes (Wang, 2001). Moreover, participation in policy encourages diversity and inclusion of many in the process (Quick & Bryson, 2022), which fits the idea that decision-makers want to learn from others to satisfy their curiosity about the world.

As an organization, NASA has struggled with public participation and involvement in its actions. However, the response to the Challenger and Columbia disasters has shown that the agency is willing to share its failures with the public. More recently, the agency has expanded its openness to the public, encouraging more involvement in developing technoscientific work (Kaminski et al., 2016). Agency scientists and policymakers have labeled this process successful in promoting organizational innovation and improving outcomes. This is applying curiosity at the organizational level to encourage learning how the world works and improving outcomes, governance, and overall democratic performance. However, as we see in the next section, not all organizations practice these features of curiosity.

Organizations Lacking Curiosity

An excellent way to understand curiosity at the organizational level of analysis is to examine the features of agencies that struggle to achieve their goals and keep happy and effective workforces in place.

The Centers for Disease Control and Prevention and COVID

First, I must acknowledge the conflict of highlighting USHHS as a successful federal agency for curiosity but then include one of its subagencies, the CDC, as an example of an agency lacking curiosity. This is an example of how the home department does not determine the culture and features of all its parts. Moreover, it is an example of how a significant pressure, the COVID pandemic, can push an agency into not being curious. The CDC's workforce fits in many of the features of curiosity described in this book, such as being well educated and focusing on knowing how the world works. However, during the COVID pandemic, political, professional, and structural pressures led to the agency not practicing curiosity in its response to the crisis. Politically,

Trump administration engaged in unprecedented political interference with the CDC. Professionally, the CDC was focused on advancing knowledge through peer-review processes and was not as equipped as was once thought to respond to an ongoing pandemic. The CDC's mishandling of the development of testing for COVID is an example of this professional failure. Structurally, the CDC is limited to many federal agencies in our federal system, where the national government shares authority with the state governments over health-related issues and public emergency powers. The U.S. public health response system is comprised of thousands of local public health organizations, with the CDC limited in its authority to direct those local agencies. These factors hindered the CDC's ability to objectively find answers and respond to the COVID crisis more effectively.

U.S. Department of Homeland Security

The department's workforce consistently rates the work environment as being poor. It has ranked last in most of the recent Great Places to Work surveys conducted by the OPM (Davidson, 2022). The department also struggles to implement policy and promote the values of curiosity. The limitations of politics, professional factors, and structure can be used to explain these failures. Politically, the department has been in conflict since its creation when Democrats and Republicans debated the workforce's employment protections. During the Trump's Administration, the department was asked in many ways to take extra-constitutional actions through the Muslim travel ban, border control, and other troubling initiatives. Professionally, the agencies comprising the department struggle with organizational culture promoting bad behavior and outcomes. For example, Customs and Border Protection often abuses civil liberties and, like many other law enforcement agencies in the U.S., promotes a culture of unprofessionalism that makes it difficult to reform aggressive and illegal behaviors by their workforces. Structurally, the department was created in the haze of post-9/11 Washington D.C. The agencies that comprise the department often conflict with one another and hamper the overall goal of the department's creation in streamlining decision-making for policymakers.

A Framework for Studying Curiosity in Public Organizations

While the previous chapters have focused on curiosity at the individual level, whether practitioners or academics, this chapter has sought to build a framework for studying curiosity at the organizational level, particularly public organizations. Reviewing some of the features of public organizations viewed as great places to work, we can identify a few variables and commonalities that fit within the explanation of administrative curiosity developed so far in this book. Those workplace features emphasize education among employees, creativity,

Table 6.1 A Framework of Administrative Curiosity for Public Organizations

Variables of curious organizations	Behaviors of curious organizations
Educated workforces Creativity Diversity Mission-orientation Respect for public involvement	Adaption Empathy Caring

Source: Created by the author

diversity, a focus on mission and outcomes, and respect for public involvement. These features lead to curiosity in organizations and produce certain positive behaviors in organizations.

The book also examines how curiosity affects overall public organizations. This part of the research is meant to show how the actions of curious public managers can influence a public organization. To understand the features of curious public organizations, I have used the following hypotheses to guide my examinations of agencies that may demonstrate curiosity.

Hypothesis 1: Curious public organizations demonstrate adaptive learning
Hypothesis 2: Curious public organizations demonstrate empathy.
Hypothesis 3: Curious public organizations demonstrate caring.

1. Adaptive Learning

This chapter has examined successful organizations to help identify features of curiosity, and it can be asserted that agencies encouraging diversity of opinion, creativity, and public involvement are well suited for adaptive learning. Moreover, administrative curiosity, defined as seeking how the world works to make informed decisions, is adaptive learning. As noted in Chapter 4, Moynihan and Landuty (2009) have argued for "learning forums" in public organizations. The authors' idea of learning forums fits within this book's overall focus on administrative curiosity and could be an ideal component of public organizations that are curious about the world and, therefore, can be adaptive.

2. Empathetic Organizations

The organizations discussed in this chapter that demonstrate curiosity can also be considered ones that emphasize the citizens they serve. How do we dedicate empathy within public organizations? From her study of the Housing Authority of Baltimore, Dolamore (2019) provides a helpful framework. Empathy in an organization's culture can be dedicated by asking questions related to the following categories: physical characteristics and general

environment; policies, procedures, and structures; socialization; leadership behavior; rewards and recognition; discourse; and lastly, learning and performance
(p. 8).

Empathy is essential to public service. In a world of standard operating procedures, bureaucrats or public administrators need to empathize with the individuals they serve. Some authors have viewed empathy as crucial to the future of
public administration, and I agree. For instance, Meyer et al. (2022) have called
for replacing the traditional measures of outcomes in public administration—
efficiency, effectiveness, and equity—with *empathy*, engagement, equity, and ethics. Through these new measures and guideposts, public administrators may approach their service in a manner that lessens disparities in the communities and
help them "understand the complexities of the diverse world" (Meyer et al., 2022,
p. 355). This is empathy in action, and it leads to curiosity. In fact, I would argue
that these four new E's of public administration are only possible if public administrators practice the connecting glue of curiosity.

Are faculty in public administration programs teaching empathy? In the
previous chapter, we examined how NASPAA faculty are teaching curiosity.
We found limitations in how faculty teach the concept. In effect, most viewed
the concept as important, but some doubted how it could be taught, and the
examples of exercises show this limitation. Edlins and Dolamore (2018) found
similar results when they surveyed public administration faculty about how
they view empathy and teach the concept. They found that academic programs in public administration may not teach empathy as much as would be
thought, and the authors called for more discussion on how to teach the important topic. I agree, and the same can be said for curiosity. Again, curiosity
and empathy go hand-in-hand. Empathy can be taught through exercises focusing on curiosity, because to truly get to the bottom of how something works,
individuals need to put themselves in the shoes of others or practice empathy.

Moreover, organizations need to do the same. Empathetic culture in
organizations leads to them wanting to know how the world works and being
more likely to care about the individuals being served by the public programs.

3. Caring Organizations

In an essay in *Public Voices* (2020), I argue how caring organizations help
employees fight against burnout, lessen workplace bullying, and are more
effective, efficient, and fair overall. As we see in this chapter's discussion of
curiosity focusing on the organizational level, caring encourages curiosity
throughout an organization. Caring organizations want to know about their employees, even if leaders may not always like the answers that they get. Caring
organizations seek to know how the world works so they can do their best to
support those they serve.

Most scholarly work on caring organizations comes from health-related
fields, such as medicine, psychology, and social work. However, in recent

years, there has been more of a focus on caring in private organizations that are coming to realize the economic value of such working environments. A clear definition of caring organizations comes from psychology. According to Fuqua and Newman (2002), caring organizations are "systems where the personal concern about the welfare of others is the norm" (p. 134). As the authors argue, caring culture in an organization can be cultivated by focusing on gratitude, forgiveness, encouragement, compassion, sensitivity, community, tolerance, charity, and inclusion. Curiosity can be thought of as the glue that brings these practices together. To care about others, one needs to be curious about their lives. So, in effect, curious organizations are caring ones, and caring organizations are comprised of curious individuals. In the public sector, the curious public administrator concerns herself with helping create caring organizations.

How and where do organizations show that they care? The extent to which an organization is caring can be seen in a few places and a few actions of the agency. Noddings (2015) astutely notes that caring organizations show it in their public statements and policies. These policies include fighting against harassment and bullying, empowering employees, promoting fairness, advancing diversity and inclusion, and other policies and practices that seek to make an organization a place where employees feel safe, rewarded and accepted. Simply put, these policies are first communicated through what organizations say in their mission statement about how they value their employees. It is the first step toward effective action.

Here is an example of a mission statement that stresses the value of the organization's employees. The statement is an example used by the Society for Human Resource Management (2023).

> Department of Commerce Office of Human Resources Management
> To develop and manage value-added human resources policies and programs, and provide expert consultation, services and solutions in an efficient and customer-focused manner; and to provide our employees with the tools necessary to meet our customers' needs. We are committed to the fair selection and development of our diverse workforce.

Importantly, caring organizations demonstrate care in their work environments and practices. Organizations need to follow up on caring mission statements with caring practices. Organizations, such as honestly many in higher education, can have the loftiest public statements and policies focusing on promoting care. Still, in practice, these places may be environments that promote the opposite of care, such as abuse, bullying, discrimination, and administrative evil. To be caring, organizations need to practice what they preach. These organizations should have low levels of turnover, little to no discriminatory actions brought against them, supportive workplaces and managers, and other characteristics that demonstrate that they actually care about their workers and not just say they care. These places are often the ones that succeed economically.

In public administration, the focus of care can, in many ways, be traced back to the great theorist Mary Parker Follett and her emphasis on relational administration (Burnier, 2003). The relational leader focuses on "care ethics" in their organization to ensure the concerns of workers and the people served (Burnier, 2003). As Burnier (2009) has termed it, there needs to be this "care-centered" approach in public administration, which is not dependent on market forces. In the public sector, caring organizations should be the norm. The focus is on taking care of communities, and public organizations should also take care of their workers (Burnier, 2009). And to be effective, organizations need to take care of their workers first and then the individuals they serve. Uncaring organizations are not empathetic, effective, and fair places to work.

But achieving caring organizations requires refocusing how we measure performance away from market mechanisms (Burnier, 2009) to more holistic evaluation practices (Burnier, 2018) concerned with outcomes that promote democratic values. To push our public organizations away from market mechanisms, I have argued that there is a need for curiosity, so again, the glue that holds together the caring organization and its focus on the welfare of others and, in public administration, democratic values, is having administrators who practice curiosity.

Concluding Thoughts on Curiosity in Organizations

This chapter has sought to examine curiosity at the organizational level in public administration. It has done so by identifying features of curiosity in federal agencies where individuals are happy to work. The analysis then used these features to develop a starting framework for exploring curious organizations. From this, I identified three hypotheses for describing curious organizations and discussed these areas: adaptive learning, empathy, and caring.

Future research needs to explore these hypotheses in greater detail. This chapter is simply the start to this future work on examining curiosity at the organizational level. Nevertheless, for this book, it is vital to build the theory of administrative curiosity, which is primarily focused on the individual level, explored in Chapters 4 and 5. But, of course, organizations are populated by individuals. Those individual-level features and practices of curiosity work their way up to affect the entire organization, and agencies where people are succeeding, solving problems, and happy, and other positive features can often be ones with public servants practicing curiosity in their daily work. These curious organizations should be adaptive, empathetic, and caring, which all are needed features for a future administration that is effective, democratic, and fair. This is no small task, indeed, but it starts with curiosity at the individual level.

Note

1 For more information, see: https://bestplacestowork.org/rankings/detail/?c=OM00

References

Alkadry, M. G., Blessett, B., & Patterson, V. L. (2017). Public administration, diversity, and the ethic of getting things done. *Administration & Society, 49*(8), 1191–1218.

Burnier, D. (2003). Other voices/other rooms: Towards a care-centered public administration. *Administrative Theory & Praxis, 25*(4), 529–544.

Burnier, D. (2009). Markets no more: Toward a care-centered public administration. *Administrative Theory & Praxis, 31*(3), 396–402.

Burnier, D. (2018). Reimagining performance in public administration theory and practice: Creating a democratic performativity of care and hope. *Administrative Theory & Praxis, 40*(1), 62–78.

Cates, C. (1979). Beyond muddling: Creativity. *Public Administration Review, 39*(6), 527–532.

Davidson, J. (2022). Federal employees are not happy. These agencies are especially troubled. *Washington Post*. Retrieved from www.washingtonpost.com/politics/2022/07/13/best-in-government-survey-poor-satisfaction-employees/

Dolamore, S. (2019). Detecting empathy in public organizations: Creating a more relational public administration. *Administrative Theory & Praxis*, 1–24.

Edlins, M., & Dolamore, S. (2018). Ready to serve the public? The role of empathy in public service education programs. *Journal of Public Affairs Education, 24*(3), 300–320.

Eldor, L., & Harpaz, I. (2019). The nature of learning climate in public administration: A cross-sectorial examination of its relationship with employee job involvement, proactivity, and creativity. *The American Review of Public Administration, 49*(4), 425–440.

Fuqua, D. R., & Newman, J. L. (2002). Creating caring organizations. *Consulting Psychology Journal: Practice and Research, 54*(2), 131.

Goodsell, C. T. (2010). *Mission mystique: Belief systems in public agencies.* Sage.

Houtgraaf, G., Kruyen, P. M., & van Thiel, S. (2023). Public sector creativity as the origin of public sector innovation: A taxonomy and future research agenda. *Public Administration, 101*(2), 539–556.

Inan, I. (2013). *The philosophy of curiosity.* Routledge.

Kaminski, A., Buquo, L., Roman, M. C., Beck, B., & Thaller, M. (2016). NASA's public participation universe: Why and how the US space agency is democratizing its approaches to innovation. In *AIAA space 2016.* Aerospace Research Center. (p. 5466).

McGregor, D. (1960). Theory X and theory Y. *Organization Theory, 358*(374), 5.

Meyer, S. J., Johnson III, R. G., & McCandless, S. (2022). Meet the new Es: Empathy, engagement, equity, and ethics in public administration. *Public Integrity, 24*(4–5), 353–363.

Moynihan, D. P., & Landuyt, N. (2009). How do public organizations learn? Bridging cultural and structural perspectives. *Public Administration Review, 69*(6), 1097–1105.

NASA. (2021). *Agency science workforce study phase 1 report.* Retrieved from https://science.nasa.gov/files/atoms/files/FINAL%20Agency%20Science%20Workforce%20Study%2003.02.pdf

Partnership for Public Service. (2020). *Best places to work in the federal government.* Retrieved from https://bestplacestowork.org/rankings/detail/?c=OM00

Quick, K. S., & Bryson, J. M. (2022). Public participation. In *Handbook on theories of governance* (pp. 158–168). Edward Elgar Publishing.

Rangarajan, N. (2008). Evidence of different types of creativity in government: A multimethod assessment. *Public Performance & Management Review, 32*(1), 132–163.

Society of Human Resource Management. (2023). *Human resources mission statement examples.* Retrieved from www.shrm.org/resourcesandtools/tools-and-samples/policies/pages/missionstatementhr.aspx

U.S. Office of Personnel Management (OPM). (2017). *Common characteristics of the government.* Retrieved from www.opm.gov/policy-data-oversight/data-analysis-documentation/federal-employment-reports/common-characteristics-of-the-government/ccog2017.pdf

U.S. Office of Personnel Management (OPM). (2022). *FedScope.* Retrieved from www.fedscope.opm.gov/employment.asp

Unsworth, K. (2001). Unpacking creativity. *Academy of Management Review, 26*(2), 289–297.

Wang, X. (2001). Assessing public participation in US cities. *Public Performance & Management Review, 24*(4), 322–336.

West, J. P., & Berman, E. M. (1997). Administrative creativity in local government. *Public Productivity & Management Review,* 446–458.

7 Insatiable Curiosity—An Administrative Theory for the Public Sector Workplace

Curiosity should be thought of as a foundational feature of an effective public servant, or as Louis Brownlow argued, "[T]he principal requirement of a good administrator is an insatiable curiosity" (Stone, 1981, p. 507). Curiosity, thus, was once viewed as a foundational component of being an effective public administrator and the first step toward innovative government. Over the years, we have moved away from this view, and little to no attention has been paid to curiosity in public administration scholarship. During this time, psychology, philosophy, medicine, and management have advanced knowledge of curiosity in the workplace. Public administration has advanced our understanding of innovation in government (De Vries et al., 2016), but there has been little attention to the first step in innovation, the curiosity of public servants. This book extends this research to the public sector and calls for a return to viewing curiosity as the main requirement of an effective public servant. Such a return will include the development of a new doctrine for the field (Hatcher, 2019)—a doctrine that promotes empathy, exploration, knowledge-building, and other learning activities among public administrators to encourage curiosity in their daily work.

Widespread curiosity among public administrators will bubble up to overall organizations, leading to agencies that promote public involvement in decision-making, advance diversity, and are caring in their policies and practices to their employees and the individuals that are being served. These goals are lofty, but they are needed to rebuild government in the U.S., where political corruption, restriction of fundamental freedoms, and multiple crises from pandemics to environmental degradation have led to a political system that is sliding away from a functioning democracy.

In public administration, the doctrine is needed as a focusing framework or "way of doing business" that helps advance research and practice. Current theoretical frameworks either lead us in the wrong direction toward unfettered market mechanisms (e.g., New Public Management) or lack the appropriate guiding concept that curiosity provides, which is an elegant and straightforward foundation for the doctrine, calling for public administrators to objectively seek to learn how the world works and in turn improve their decision-making.

DOI: 10.4324/9781032668826-7

Insatiable curiosity can be the guidepost that moves theory, research, and practice forward. To do this, we need to understand how practitioners view the concept, how faculty can teach administrators to embrace insatiable curiosity, and how public organizations can be improved by following the guidepost. This short book has tried to accomplish a lot to promote curiosity and use it to help explain what we do and study in public administration. The book has tried to do the following.

- First, develop a definition of curiosity appropriate for the public sector.
- Second, develop a theory of administrative curiosity.
- Third, test this theory at the individual level by surveying practitioners (i.e., city managers) and academics (i.e., NASPAA faculty).
- Fourth, examine this theory at the organizational level by discussing some of the variables of successful public agencies and some of the aspects of agencies that do not demonstrate features of curiosity.
- Lastly, in this chapter, I bring everything together to reassess the administrative theory of curiosity, and I examine the big picture for curiosity and administration by discussing ideas for future research and practice. Hopefully, the findings and discussions in this book will encourage curious public administrators.

What Have We Learned?

The book has developed an administrative theory of curiosity and examined it by surveying city managers and administrators, surveying NASPAA faculty, and thinking about the theory would work at the organizational level. Through the book's chapters and analyses, we have learned the following.

1. Curious Public Administrators

Public administrators are highly curious, and even more so than private sector managers. They tend to group into two main clusters of curiosity, a large majority demonstrating curiosity and a much small group expressing caution when interacting with others in the search for knowledge. From the results of this chapter, though, we can make some general conclusions about how the book's theory of the curious public administrator applies to city managers. Most surveyed city managers and administrators were sorted into a grouping called *Curious Public Administrators*. These public administrators demonstrated strong opinion support for working on novel problems, investigating these issues in-depth, and working with others to seek an objective answer to how to address these programs. Interestingly, a few public administrators cautioned against curiosity concepts and worked with others to seek solutions to work-related problems.

When comparing the results of this book's survey results to city managers and administrators to surveys distributed by the M-Workplace Curiosity Scale to private sector managers (Kashdan et al., 2020), public sector managers appear to demonstrate higher levels of curiosity. Next, I analyzed the opinion data of the city managers and administrators using regression modeling. The analyses found, interestingly, no statistical differences. Gender, race, education, size of their cities, and other factors did not predict if managers were more curious in the public workplace. However, an interesting finding came from the analysis that public administrators leading smaller cities were likelier to express stronger support for curiosity in their work.

2. Curious Public Administration Faculty

Public administration faculty are highly curious and hold the opinion that the concept can be taught in the classroom and our programs, with a small group having the view that the concept cannot be taught. The faculty detailed a wealth of information on assignments that will help promote curiosity and their ideas on where the concept should be taught in the public administration curriculum. However, a small grouping of faculty held strongly that curiosity could not be taught in the public administration classroom. These faculty respondents talked about curiosity as a trait, not a skill that can be learned in the classroom. Considering curiosity as a trait and not a teachable skill is dangerously close to the notion that other areas cannot be taught, such as proficiency in math being a trait and not a skill (Hatfield et al., 2022). It should be stressed that this opinion is not widely shared throughout the statements made by public administration faculty, but it is an important critique of teaching curiosity. The viewpoint is that certain aspects of administration are personal traits that cannot be taught.

3. Curious Public Organizations

Successful organizations can adapt, and they adapt through curiosity. Curious organizations may be agencies that promote fairness, caring, empathy, education, diversity of individuals and opinions, and creativity, leading to adaptative learning. This chapter reviewed federal agencies where employees are happy with their jobs and workplaces. The analysis then used these features to develop a framework for exploring curious organizations through adaptive learning, empathy, and caring. The book starts a discussion regarding curiosity at the organizational level. This book has been mostly concerned with curiosity in the public workplace at the individual level. Nevertheless, organizations are populated by individuals, and future research into curiosity and public administration needs to explore the concept at both the individual and organizational levels.

Where Does This Fit in Public Administration Theory and Practice?

In Chapter 3, I constructed a theory of curiosity for public administrators. The theory is based on the theories and research reviewed in Chapters 1 and 2. The theory holds assumptions about how curious public administrators approach their work.

- First, they are knowledge seekers and are intrinsically motivated to find it.
- Second, they practice empathy in the workplace.
- Third, seeking knowledge and practicing empathy help curious administrators care about their colleagues and the people they serve.
- Lastly, seeking knowledge, practicing empathy, and demonstrating caring lead curious administrators to be better learners than managers who lack curiosity, leading to learning and adaptive public organizations.

From these assumptions, specific hypotheses can be constructed to examine curiosity in the public workplace and how public administration faculty teach the concept. Next, I recap these hypotheses and discuss what the book's analyses found. First, I discuss the hypothesis concerning how public administrators view curiosity in public workplaces.

Hypothesis 1: Curious public administrators are more likely to view the objective search for knowledge as a crucial part of their jobs than other parts of their work.

The analyses in Chapter 4 demonstrated that public administrators express support for joyful exploration in their work and the need to focus on objective learning to be effective in their positions.

Hypothesis 2: Curious public administrators are more likely to express the importance of practicing empathy as a part of their jobs, compared to other parts of their work.

The analysis in Chapter 4 found that public administrators recognized the importance of empathy in their work, holding opinions that strongly support this assumption. For instance, most of the surveyed city managers and administrators strongly agreed or agreed with this statement, "Public administrators need to empathize with all members of their community."

Hypothesis 3: Curious public administrators are more likely to express the importance of demonstrating caring behaviors as part of their jobs, compared to other parts of their work.

The analysis in Chapter 4 showed that public administrators strongly supported the caring aspects of their jobs. Most of the surveyed city managers and administrators strongly agreed or agreed with this statement, "Public administrators need to practice compassion in their work."

Hypothesis 4: Curious public administrators are more likely to express the importance of learning, not just searching for knowledge, as part of their jobs, compared to other parts of their work.

The opinions expressed by public administrators when completing the curiosity index used in this book demonstrate that most held a strong view that curiosity should be practiced in public workplaces.

Chapter 5 moved to analyze a set of theoretical questions regarding how public administration faculty define curiosity and teach it in the classroom. These questions and the book's findings are summarized next.

What do public affairs faculty think about the features of curiosity?
What do public affairs faculty think about the importance of the features of curiosity compared to other areas of information?
How do public affairs faculty define curiosity?
How do public affairs faculty teach curiosity in their classrooms?
Are there differences between the faculty who view curiosity as vital and those who do not see it as important?

Public administration faculty view curiosity as a vital concept of effective administration, but they have various definitions. The definitions shared some commonalities with this book's focus on curiosity as objectively learning how the world works. Most faculty felt that curiosity should and can be taught in the public administration classroom. A small group of the surveyed faculty was cautious about whether curiosity can be taught in the classroom, but it can be argued that they wrongly view curiosity as a trait and not a skill that can be learned. There were few differences between the groups that viewed curiosity as a teachable concept and those that expressed caution. Interestingly, OLS regression analysis did show statistical support that faculty who reported serving as administrators were more likely to view curiosity as teachable, compared to faculty who have not held administrative positions.

A Research Agenda for Insatiable Curiosity

The book has found evidence that practicing public administrators view curiosity as an important component of the public workplace. Additionally, faculty expressed strong support for curiosity in their workplace of the public administration classroom, and they provided, as detailed in Chapter 5, multiple useful examples of assignments and curriculum changes to put in place to teach public servants the importance of curiosity in their work. We have used the literature reviewed and empirical findings in this book to build a theory of the curious public administrator. Next, we as a field must continue working on a research agenda to study insatiable curiosity in public administration. What would this research agenda include? First, Chapter 6 of this book started a discussion on the features of curiosity at the organizational level. Future research in this area needs to be conducted. Second, the book's main empirical contributions can be found in Chapters 5 and 6. This part of the book represents the first time a standardized instrument of workplace curiosity has been administrated to public sector employees and faculty. Future scholarship needs to administrate the curiosity instruments to public employees in different types of positions at different levels of government. For instance, work can explore the opinions of state public managers and federal bureaucrats and compare their opinions to those of the municipal public managers studied in this book and the opinion of private sector managers. This work needs to be followed up with more in-depth interviewing and case studies of curiosity in the public workplace and among public administrators, organizations, and faculty. This will take work, though, and multiple research projects beyond this book.

The Curious Public Administrator: A Needed New Doctrine

We started this book with an argument for the curious public administrator as a new theoretical doctrine to help guide public administration through troubling times. And these times are troubling indeed. Objective observers of the recent public administration in the U.S. should be able to recognize the damage that a president lacking curiosity can cause. Having leaders who are not seeking multiple opinions, are failing to explore their personal intellectual growth, and are holding onto dogmatic views that may not fit reality is damaging to public administration and dangerous for the future of democratic governance. Something as simple as being curious about the world around oneself pushes one toward self-reflection. Moreover, such curiosity may move public administrations beyond reflection to critical reflexivity in their work, leading to a transformative approach to government (Cunliffe & Jun, 2005). Troubling times call for transformative approaches and not marginal improvements, and being motivated by curiosity offers a possible path to the transformation of public administration.

References

Cunliffe, A. L., & Jun, J. S. (2005). The need for reflexivity in public administration. *Administration & Society, 37*(2), 225–242.

De Vries, H., Bekkers, V., & Tummers, L. (2016). Innovation in the public sector: A systematic review and future research agenda. *Public Administration, 94*(1), 146–166.

Hatcher, W. (2019). The curious public administrator: The new administrative doctrine. *Public Integrity, 21*(3), 225–228.

Hatfield, N., Brown, N., & Topaz, C. M. (2022). Do introductory courses disproportionately drive minoritized students out of STEM pathways? *PNAS Nexus, 1*(4), 167.

Stone, D. C. (1981). Innovative organizations require innovative managers. *Public Administration Review, 41*(5), 507–513.

Index

Note: Page numbers in **bold** indicate a table on the corresponding page.

For Product Safety Concerns and Information please contact our EU
representative GPSR@taylorandfrancis.com
Taylor & Francis Verlag GmbH, Kaufingerstraße 24, 80331 München, Germany